Entertaining Angels

Entertaining Angels

A Guide to Heaven for Atheists and True Believers

F. Forrester Church

1817

Harper & Row, Publishers, San Francisco

Cambridge, Hagerstown, New York, Philadelphia, Washington
London, Mexico City, São Paulo, Singapore, Sydney

FIRST EDITION

Library of Congress Cataloging-in-Publication Data

Church, F. Forrester.
　Entertaining angels.

　1. Angels—Anecdotes, facetiae, satire, etc.
I. Title.
BT966.2.C49　1987　　235'.3　　86-43000
ISBN 0-06-061372-6

87　88　89　90　91　HC　10　9　8　7　6　5　4　3　2　1

For Amy

Contents

Preface

When I was eight years old, my friends and I joined the Cub Scouts. Fortunately, my memory is such that most of the details marking my two years of service are forever lost to me. I remember only a few salient points. When we enlisted in the Scouts, all our uniforms looked the same—midnight blue with gold trim. By the time I applied for and received an honorable discharge, you wouldn't have known that I and my fellows were part of the same troop. Proof of this was emblazoned all over our uniforms. Mine was still midnight blue with gold trim. Theirs were like Joseph's proverbial coat of many colors. In fact, I earned only one merit badge as a scout. Not a rampant lion, or a barbell, or a fish, or a tent, or a deer, but a needle and thread. My sole accomplishment during two years of scouting was to weave a potholder for my grandmother.

There you have them: my credentials for writing this book. I'll spare you the details, but however you cut it, I couldn't possibly afford to be a perfectionist. Which is why I find angels so congenial. Angels aren't perfectionists either. As G. K. Chesterton said, "Angels can fly because they take themselves lightly."* In contrast, the devil—aspiring to perfection—fell on account of his gravity.

This guide to heaven is the second volume of three, a sequel and companion piece to *The Devil & Dr. Church,*

---

*Sources for quotations are listed at the end of this book.

my little book on hell. I approach it—heaven, that is—with some trepidation. For most of us evil holds a terrible fascination, in contrast to which goodness is often mistaken for something fusty and prim. At their readers' peril, far greater authors than I have discovered this. After all, we remember John Milton for *Paradise Lost,* not *Paradise Regained.*

William Blake offers this explanation: "The reason Milton wrote in fetters when he wrote of Angels and God, and at liberty when of Devils and Hell, is because he was a true poet, and of the Devil's party without knowing it." In Blake's estimation, this is a compliment. That's because Blake underestimated angels; this despite his brilliance, even despite having seen them with his own two eyes in the trees outside his window when he was a boy of seven. Blake accused angels of having no sense of humor. Yet surely they are nothing if not humorous. Eternal bliss would be a sorry state indeed if this were not the case. In fact, it is in their nature to be entertaining, highly entertaining. But as Abraham discovered in Mamre and the Epistle to the Hebrews reminds us, "Some have entertained angels unawares" (Heb. 13:2).

Both in Hebrew and in Greek, "angel" means messenger, a messenger of God. The word is indicative of duty, not of nature. An angel is what it says and does, not what it is. On the other hand, one of the reasons angels are so elusive is that in their case the medium truly is the message. The message and the medium are God. "That's all an angel is," wrote Meister Eckhart, "an idea of God."

Quite a leap from the angels of today! Pink-faced cherubs with mouths agape, Hallmark choristers singing Noel on the mantel at Christmastime. My wife, Amy, has collected angels, two every Christmas, ever since she was a little girl. My favorite, and hers, is a singular fat porcelain angel wearing a dashiki. She gives a hint of what angels are like— startling, amusing, and slightly disorienting—but it is only a hint.

My hope is to offer a few more. I shall first survey heaven as popularly depicted, testing its toxicity for angels and for humans. After exploring idolatry, both personal and corporate, I'll then introduce the angel as stranger—unbidden, unexpected, and unlikely. The heart of the book will be spun from the stuff of paradox, how we harrow heaven, and how what we hope for has already come to pass without our noticing.

My thesis is a simple one. If angels come in packages we'd almost always pick the wrong one. Even as the devil is evil disguised as good, angels are goodness disguised. They show up in foolscap, calico and gingham, and brown paper bags. Jesus discovered the realm of God in a mustard seed, the smallest and least portentous of all seeds. Mustard seeds and angels have this in common. They are little epiphanies of the divine amidst the ordinary.

As with my book on the devil, the following essay on angels—on heaven and the good—is addressed both to atheists and true believers. Unless we learn to discriminate between our own narrow good and good in the larger sense, whether common or divine, all of us and the earth we share are doomed. "The word good has many meanings," as Chesterton also said. "For example if a man were to shoot his grandmother at a range of five hundred yards, I should call him a good shot, but not necessarily a good man."

I am a religious liberal. Ever since the Reformation, we religious liberals have been conducting a theological search-and-destroy mission, its purpose being to strip away the trappings of religion, the mystagogy and priestcraft, in an attempt to restore to faith its intellectual and ethical integrity. In some ways it is a little like trying to find the seed of an onion by peeling away its layers. Eventually, nothing is left but our tears.

I am no fan of mystagogy and priestcraft, but neither am I at all convinced that by dint of sheer rationality we can come even close to understanding the mystery of being alive and having to die. Life is a miracle that can't be explained without explaining it away. Our most profound encounters lead inexorably from the rational to the trans-rational realm. Yet myth, parable, and paradox—our only tools for enlightenment here—are the very tools we religious liberals have seen fit to lock away. That they are blunted through misuse by biblical literalists takes nothing from their original edge. They can be polished and put to new use.

By remythologizing humanism, in no way do I mean to suggest that humanism itself is outdated. Grounded in experience rather than revelation, with the mind its only oracle, humanism has always been a salutary corrective to tyranny and bondage, whether religious or political. Fundamentalism, with its absolute truth claims, is incompatible not only with the free exercise of reason, but also with pluralism, the preservation of which is essential if we are to survive as neighbors on this tiny planet. The greatest danger we face is competing ideologies, closed systems that inspire hatred in the name of Truth or God. Neither is ours to claim, at least not with exclusive title. We know so little and learn so slowly. Others have to be protected from us.

My own theology is a form of Christian Universalism—Universalism modified by Christianity, not the other way around. Universalism can be perverted in two ways. One is to elevate one truth into a universal truth ("My church is the one true church"); the other is to reduce distinctive truths to a lowest common denominator ("All religion is merely a set of variations upon the golden rule"). The Universalism I embrace does neither. It holds that the same light shines through all our windows, but each window is different. The windows modify the light, even as Christianity does my Universalism, refracting it in a myriad of ways, shaping it in different patterns, suggesting different meanings.

Fundamentalists, whatever their persuasion, claim that the light shines through their window only. Skeptics draw the opposite conclusion. Seeing the bewildering variety of windows and observing the folly of the worshipers, they conclude that there is no light. But the windows are not the light. The whole light—God, Truth—is beyond our perceiving. God is veiled. Some people have trouble believing in a God who looks into any eyes but theirs. Others have trouble believing in a God they cannot see. But that none of us can look directly into God's eyes certainly doesn't mean God isn't there, mysterious, unknowable, gazing into ours.

One final thing. Though the light of God is refracted through our windows in many distinctive ways, when the time comes for us to die, the same sun sets on each of our horizons. This we *should* be able to perceive. The principle challenge of theology today is to provide symbols and metaphors that will bring us, in all our glorious diversity, into closer kinship with one another as sons and daughters of life and death.

A word of thanks to Clayton E. Carlson, vice president and publisher of Harper & Row, San Francisco, for continuing to encourage me to play with theology in my own peculiar way, and to Terry Mulry, first-year student at Harvard Divinity School, whose help and advice have proved invaluable. My brother-in-law, Donald Brenneis, and my friends, Debra Berger and James Jarnagin, read the manuscript, making many wonderful suggestions. And my parents-in-law, Gordon and Nina Furth, provided a heavenly setting (just south of "the city of the angels") in which to spend a summer writing.

This book is dedicated to Amy, my wife of seventeen years. In addition to bolstering me in many precious ways, blessedly, in terms of my own understanding of the good, she lives up to the model of ministerial wife as encapsulated in this vignette courtesy of my colleague Frank Schulman. One day Frank delivered a particularly brilliant sermon. Upon returning home after church, Frank asked his wife, "How many really great preachers do you think there are in this denomination?" "One fewer than you think there are," she replied.

1. Heaven as Hell: Harps, Hymnals, and Halos

I want to be an angel
And with the angels stand
A crown upon my forehead,
A harp within my hand.

URANIA BAILEY

The angels all were singing out of tune
And hoarse with having little else to do,
Excepting to wind up the sun and moon,
Or curb a runaway young star or two.

LORD BYRON

When Captain Stormfield marched into heaven, he was in for a mighty surprise. Yes, he was met by St. Peter. Things were in order as far as that was concerned. The problem was, as Stormfield perceived it and Mark Twin reported it, Peter was out to lunch.

"I beg pardon, and you mustn't mind my reminding you and seeming to meddle," Stormfield says to Peter, "but hain't you forgot something?" Peter ponders for a moment and then shakes his head. "Forgot something? No, not that I know of." Stormfield is stunned. "Think," he says. So Peter thinks, but he has to admit, "No, I can't seem to have forgot anything."

Put yourself in Captain Stormfield's shoes. After more than a thousand church services, many devoted to the advantages of heaven over earth, a truly good man arrives at the Pearly Gates and the gatekeeper doesn't seem to know what in the world heaven is all about.

Think about it.

If you were doing a crossword puzzle, and the clue was "heavenly item," four letters, first letter "h," there would be only two obvious possibilities, halo and harp.

"Look at me," Captain Stormfield complains, "look at me all over." Peter looks. "Well?" he asks. "Well!" Stormfield cries, "You don't notice anything? If I branched out amongst the elect looking like this, wouldn't I attract considerable attention? Wouldn't I be a little conspicuous?"

Peter is nonplussed. "I don't see anything the matter. What do you lack?"

"Lack! Why, I lack my harp, and my wreath, and my halo, and my hymn-book, and my palm branch—I lack everything that a body naturally requires up here, my friend."

As amazing as it may seem, the gatekeeper of heaven is truly puzzled by all this. After pondering for a while, Peter finally says, "Well, you seem to be a curiosity every way a body takes you. I never heard of these things before."

Captain Stormfield looks at St. Peter in astonishment. Then he puts it on the line. "Now, I hope you don't take it as an offense, for I don't mean any, but really, for a man that has been in the Kingdom as long as I reckon you have, you do seem to know powerful little about its customs."

That's the problem with heaven. We know more about it than the angels do. A vacation forever, Sunday seven days a week, everyone in uniform, harps, hymnals, and halos commissioned upon arrival from the PX, not to mention wings. Robert Louis Stevenson once wrote that "to equip a dull, respectable person with wings would be a parody of an angel." Fortunately angels have a sense of humor.

So did Mark Twain.

You'll have to get the whole story from Twain himself; but, in short, to please Captain Stormfield and free the Pearly Gates for other arrivals, Peter gave in to his request and provided him with a harp, a wreath, a halo, a hymnbook, and a palm branch. At last, fully equipped and in a state of absolute bliss, the good captain settled down on a cloud with about a million other angels, gave his palm branch a wave or two for luck, tuned up his harp strings and started to sing.

About seventeen hours later, the angel next to him asks, "Don't you know any tune but the one you've been pegging at all day?"

"Not another blessed one," says he.

"Don't you reckon you could learn another one?"

"Never, I've tried to, but I couldn't manage it."

At this, his companion shakes his unhaloed head. "It's a long time to hang to the one," he says. "Eternity, you know." To which Stormfield replies, "Don't break my heart. I'm getting low-spirited enough already."

They sit in silence next to one another. Finally, the veteran angel asks, "Are you glad to be here?" To which Captain Stormfield replies, "Old man, I'll be frank with you. This *ain't* just as near my idea of bliss as I thought it was going to be when I used to go to church."

Whatever happens after we die, I certainly hope it isn't this. So defined, heaven might best be described as punishment for good behavior. In fact, an eternity of anything would be nothing less than an intolerable bore. Just think of your favorite pastime, one you love more than anything else in the whole wide world. Imagine a millennium of lying on the beach reading a good book, or an eternal game of bridge, or having your back scratched forever. The last of these does have its possibilities, but even they would wear out long before your back did.

It is human nature to be dissatisfied with what we have. Our work, our looks, our health, our sex lives, the length of our vacations, the size of our apartments, the way we live our lives. Everywhere we run up against limits. Often, we cannot do what we dream of doing, have what we fantasize having, be who we wish to be. In an odd way, each of these limits is a reminder of our mortality, the limit that is placed upon life itself. Not that limits, even this ultimate limit, are bad. They establish value. Remember, the more scarce something is the more precious it becomes. If gold grew on trees and apples were buried deep within the ground, we would count our fortune in apples, not gold.

When King Midas turned his whole world into gold, he became poor. What once he had placed ultimate value upon turned out to be worthless the moment that he could have as much of it as he wanted whenever he wanted. That's the principal problem with our fantasy of heaven. Not only is "life without end" not what it's cracked up to be, it is precisely the opposite. Such heaven is not heaven, it is hell.

Maurice Sendak hints at this in his children's story about a pampered dog. This little dog had everything. She had her own pillows, her own comb, and her own brush. She had a red wool sweater and two wide windows through which to gaze out upon the world. She even had two bowls to eat from and a master who loved her. Despite all this, she left home, explaining, "I am discontented. I want something I do not have. There must be more to life than having everything."

How about having everything forever? Let's take a brief romp through heaven, the heaven promised in story and song to those of us who are good. I shall be playing here to the prejudices of my skeptical friends. Just keep in mind the story of the Unitarian who died and came to a fork in the road. One sign pointed to heaven and the other to a discussion on heaven. It will come as no surprise that the Unitarian chose the seminar.

First, wings.

Christian and Jewish angels are not the only ones with wings. The ancient Greeks had their winged messengers too: Hermes, postman of the Gods; and Eros, not only the carrier of love but also the idea of love, again both the messenger and the message. In fact, almost every religion has some form of intermediary commuting between the human and the divine. Which is surely why angels are depicted with wings: to facilitate their transit from heaven to earth. More a commentary on our own lack of imagination than on the true nature of angels or their needs.

Some popular theologians, not content with mere feathers, embellish their angels' wings. They armor plate them. Consider Billy Graham, who subtitles his book on angels, "God's Secret Agents." Lifting his clue from the Greek word for mighty (*dynamis*), he concludes that "angels are God's dynamite." Though Lucifer "controls one of the most powerful and well-oiled war machines in the universe," we need not fear, for "Satan's BB guns are no match for God's heavy artillery." I must confess, such assurances do not help me sleep any better at night.

What about the number of angels in heaven? Here imaginations truly soar. Unimpeded save by logic (which is not to be confused with reason), estimates run from 100,000 to more than 49 million, this latter figure divined by medieval Jewish kabbalists. Not only that, but every angel has its own name, reflective of its function. My favorite is Mefathiel, the "opener of doors," guardian angel of thieves.

And what about heaven itself? To begin with, not resting content to destroy what we love the most by supplying it in infinite quantities, when we design our heavens we indulge in an additional and even more curious form of masochism, substituting things we think we ought to desire for those we actually do.

"Man's heaven is a curious place," Mark Twain writes in his working notes for *Letters from the Earth*.

It has not a single feature in it that he values on earth. It consists wholly of diversions which on earth he cares for not at all. . . . Man's heaven is a place of reward—made it himself, mind you—all out of his own head. Very well; of the delights of *this* world man cares *most* for sexual intercourse. He will go any length for it—risk fortune, character, reputation, life itself. And what do you think he has done? In a thousand years you would never guess—*he has left it out of his heaven! Prayer takes its place.*

We do have a way of punishing ourselves for the things we most enjoy. The reason is simple: We feel guilty. When we take pleasure, or feel pleasure, something impels us to contemplate punishment. And so when we fashion our heavens, we are careful to exclude any reminder of those things that prompt even the slightest feeling of guilt. Heaven, so designed, is a negative print image. There is something perverse about this, but it tells us much less about heaven than it does about ourselves.

I am not speaking of conscience. Conscience has to do with right and wrong, not pleasure and guilt. The question is one of healthy enjoyment. It is almost as if we fear that we will be penalized somewhere down the line for every lick of pleasure we get from life. Apparently, many of us secretly believe that a good time is somehow *not* a good time. If this is so, heaven as popularly depicted may be just the ticket for everything that ails us. As one wag put it, "While it's true to say that the bulk of your time in Heaven will be taken up with praying, praying and more praying, there will be times when you feel like relaxing and consequently not enjoying yourself."

Not every image of heaven is so austere. For instance, John Milton's angels enjoy the gamut of human pleasures: warring, drinking, even making love. This latter does pose certain problems, given that in Milton's time all angels were male. As C. S. Lewis explains it (at least to his own apparent satisfaction), "An angel is, of course, always He (not She) in human language, because whether the male is, or is not, the superior sex, the masculine is certainly the superior gender."

Fortunately, at least for those crusaders for "morality" who otherwise would be condemned to an eternity of sin when they die, the question of angels being gay has been resolved. The romantic poets, most of them unabashed celebrants of heterosexual love, revealed to us that many angels—the best of them, in fact—are female. They were so successful in changing our conception of angelic gender, that today the word angel has a decidedly feminine ring.

A survey was conducted in the church school at White Bear Unitarian Church in Mahtomaedi, Minnesota. The children were asked by their minister, "What are angels like?" Bob Stow described angels as "Imaginary beings—

a cross between a bird and a boy," but he was alone in depicting them as male. His sister Jean said, "They're always women—and wonderful people." Sarah Standefer was a little more precise: "They're always girls—blond—and they wear white." But, for my money, Murray Olyphant wins the prize, describing angels as "Skinny, flat-chested girls with diaphanous robes—not very substantial." So much for sex in heaven.

It would be a shame, of course, to limit ourselves exclusively to Christian models. The Moslems, for instance, have a far more corporeal notion of heaven than most Christians do. Allowing for exaggeration and not a little hidden polemic, over the dinner table one evening Martin Luther depicted a Turkish fantasy of heaven in these words: "A beautifully set table will stand there with tasteful salvers and excellent drinks. The food will be eels and tender liver."

Even the richest of palates would weary, I'm afraid, of a constant diet of tender liver and eels. As one amusing little guide to heaven points out in its section on restaurants, "In general no matter what your taste in food may be, you can be certain that somewhere in Heaven you'll find exactly what you're looking for, even though it won't be in the least bit appetizing when you do finally track it down."

But what about music? Surely music is one consolation of heaven. One problem—a late-breaking rumor—is that Mozart didn't make it. Salieri did. For this reason among others, at least according to Edgar Allan Poe, when it comes to music Islamic angels have the edge over Christian ones. Israfel, the Mohammedan angel of music, is acclaimed by Poe (and in the Quran) for having "the most melodious voice of all God's creatures."

> None sing so wildly well
> As the angel Israfel,
> And the giddy stars (so legends tell)
> Ceasing their hymns, attend the spell
> Of his voice, all mute.

Were one to take this seriously (which surely we should not), for Christians the good news is that the trumpet will indeed sound, and sound ringingly, on Resurrection day. The bad news is that Israfel will edge out Gabriel for the honor.

One other sobering note. Though music is one of heaven's principal features, it is widely acknowledged that God gave the devil all the good tunes.

If you don't like to sing (and this should come as a particular consolation to Unitarians), you can always talk. Endlessly. One contemporary Christian writer fantasizes on how wondrous it will be to find a quiet corner somewhere in heaven and quiz Jacob about his wrestling match with the angel. "Jacob, did you expect the fight to go on as long as it did? Did you realize that would be a turning point in your life and result in a change of names?" Fortunately, if Jacob is not able to answer these questions to his own and his auditor's satisfaction, he will be able "to turn to the angels involved in case he wishes some clarification."

This writer closes by saying that "One reason heaven is going to be heaven and eternity is going to be so wonderful is that we can discuss such tremendous things as long as we wish."

I'm afraid that even I would rather sing.

The poet and philosopher Charles Erskine Scott Wood in his little book *Heavenly Discourse,* written in the late 1920s, has a much more bracing—if equally perverse—

view of conversation in heaven. Everything is turned upside down and inside out. The heretic Robert Ingersoll is master of ceremonies. Sappho, Margaret Fuller, Thomas Paine, Rabelais, and Voltaire are God's favorite interlocutors. Peter is told to stop guarding the gates, and ends up going fishing, while one religious zealot after another arrives in heaven, fails to recognize the place, and leaves.

When the stump evangelist, Billy Sunday, shows up, he is appalled to find heaven populated with sinners, publicans, and harlots. He asks God about what happened to all the souls that he sent there. "I want to tell you right here if this place isn't packed with my souls like a circus-tent on the fourth of July, it isn't the old, reliable, genuine heaven we were brought up to. Someone's been asleep at the switch."

"This is heaven, and none of your souls are here," God replies.

"They must be somewhere," the evangelist insists. "Not necessarily," says God. "The cosmos is so very large and fanatics are so infinitely small."

Billy Sunday then proposes to "convert heaven to Christianity. Have a red-hot, old-fashioned revival meeting. Run out of town all your publicans and sinners, wine-bibbers and scarlet females. No noise. No loud laughter; no singing; no drinking; no joy; all as quiet and clean as the cemetery at Gary." God instead suggests that both of them might be happier if Billy Sunday went somewhere else to mount his crusade. "Where shall I go?" Sunday asks. "I might suggest hell," God replies.

How curious it is. Following the signs toward heaven, we may end up going in the opposite direction.

To conclude this little tour of heaven, one more brief stop is necessary. Despite all his mustiness, Emanuel

Swedenborg, at once the most rationalistic and most visionary of heaven's chroniclers, makes this final telling observation in his book *Heaven and Hell*.

I have spoken with some after death who, while they lived in the world, renounced the world, . . . believing that thus they might enter the way to heaven. But these in the other life are of a sad disposition; they despise others who are not like themselves; they are indignant that they do not have a happier lot than others, believing that they merited it; they have no interest in others, and turn away from the duties of charity by which there is conjunction with heaven. They desire heaven more than others; but when they are taken up among the angels they induce anxieties that disturb the happiness of the angels; and in consequence they are sent away; and when sent away they betake themselves to desert places, where they lead a life like that which they lived in the world.

Fully to grasp this passage, you must translate it into present tense, for Swedenborg's heaven is not so much a place as it is a state of mind. "It can in no sense be said that heaven is outside of any one; it is within him . . . and a man also, so far as he receives heaven, is a recipient, a heaven, and an angel."

Here we encounter a very different heaven. Not a heaven beyond, but a heaven within; not an eternity of time, but eternity in time, expressive of joy, goodness, and service to others. Heaven can be entered only through doors that swing open and closed, not doors that are open forever.

If we pay attention, this is one thing the angels can teach us. Eternity for them is not measured in length, but in depth. Eternity is pregnant in every given moment, a quality not a quantity. When angels dance on the head of a pin, they don't concern themselves with how many can fit, as if they were crowding into a phone booth. Their full attention is devoted to the joy of the dance.

2. Why Angels Can Fly

It is not because angels are holier than men or devils that makes them angels, but because they do not expect holiness from one another, but from God alone.

WILLIAM BLAKE

Too good is bad for you.

THE TALMUD

If we were angels, almost certainly we would feel sorry for ourselves. Angels are misunderstood, ill-portrayed, trivialized, and abused even by their admirers. But angels don't feel sorry for themselves. They don't have time. And eternity is no place for a grudge. If we were to learn this, we would be more like them. It's not as presumptuous as it seems. After all, angels are not perfectionists. One was, of course, but he fell from grace.

Donald Barthelme once said, "It is a curiosity of writing about angels that, very often, one turns out to be writing about men." After all, we are only a little lower than they are. But there is this one difference. We—and I am no exception—tend to take ourselves far more seriously than angels do. It's a matter of time and eternity.

When Gulliver washed up on the Lilliputian beach, their king sent his agents to reconnoiter, instructing them to examine Gulliver carefully, and to return with a full report on any weapons he might be carrying that would jeopardize Lilliputian security. Once having pinned him down, they rifled through Gulliver's pockets. Three unusual items were unearthed, none apparently dangerous, but each decidedly foreign and therefore fascinating. The first item was a great carpet, its length and breadth sufficient to span the grand hall of the royal palace. This, of course, was Gulliver's handkerchief. The second item of interest was a mighty instrument, with poles distended from it the size of the palisades before the royal court. This was Gulliver's comb. The third item was even more baffling. Deep within the recesses of Gulliver's vestments, the king's agents discovered a great engine, one that made a noise like a waterfall, and was covered with a clear but impenetrable shield, precluding a direct examination of the monstrous figures on its face. This was Gulliver's watch.

In reporting their findings to the king, the investigators proposed that the third of these strange objects must either be a favorite pet that Gulliver brought with him from his own country, or his god—because he consulted it so often.

Eternity is not something we consult, at least not in the same sense that we do our watches. In fact, all the time in the world is nothing like it. But as with many good things and their shadows, time can masquerade as eternity. And eternity, wound up as it is with virtue, is often mocked by time.

Promptness, for instance, is a virtue. But as with every virtue, there is always the danger of too much of a good thing. I, for one, am a stickler for promptness. I arrive at airports two hours early and at dinner parties on time, which amounts to the same thing. One advantage of the latter is, while my host and hostess are changing, I have occasion to peruse the contents of their library.

Every virtue has its attendant vice. The vice attendant to promptness is not chronic lateness, it is the perfection of promptness, promptness at all cost. I stand in the door to our bathroom with my coat on, while my wife, Amy, applies her makeup.

Ministers too have been known to suffer the blandishments of a too-virtuous wife. Carrie Nation was a minister's wife. She won fame crusading against the saloon-keepers of Kansas. A domineering woman, not only did she choose her husband's subjects, but sometimes even wrote his sermons. Rumor has it that every Sunday morning, Carrie Nation sat in the front pew, coaching her husband as he preached. When she decided that he was done preaching, she would pipe up, "That will be all for today, David." If he made so bold as to go on preaching, Carrie Nation would simply mount the pulpit, close the Bible, and hand her husband his hat.

Now this was an interesting woman. She disliked smoking as much as she did drinking, and was known to punch cigars out of the mouths of men she didn't even know. She is most famous for taking her hatchet and chopping up a saloon. It can certainly be argued that if Carrie Nation had not been possessed by her passion for righteousness, she would have been a far less effective reformer than she was.

Carrie Nation was an intolerant woman. Yet even as tolerance is not always a virtue (some things deserve not tolerance, but respect, and others are so repugnant that they should not be tolerated), neither is intolerance always a vice. Vice and virtue slip in and out of one another's clothing. If practiced to perfection, any virtue can become a vice. Prudence creates niggardliness; honesty, cruelty; self-respect, vainglory; knowledge, condescension; justice, heartlessness; temperance, aridity; chastity, barrenness. In fact, there is no virtue that is not potentially an idol capable of reducing its worshipers to abject solemnity. Which is why the angels are so chary of perfectionism, even Carrie Nation's.

Several boutiques on Madison Avenue in New York City feature in their windows an exquisite crocheted pillow. It comes in several different styles, each suitable for the most elegant of divans. And in gothic or high-tech or simple contemporary lettering, it carries this message: "You can't be too rich or too thin."

Think of the insider traders on Wall Street, young men for whom half a million a year is apparently not enough. Think of the once beautiful young women with anorexia, who purge themselves of all food and whose legs are like toothpicks. Each is a tragic parody of this tongue-in-cheek message that tells us something true about ourselves and our time.

Not only *our* time. Four centuries ago, the essayist Montaigne wrote,

Who has not heard tell in Paris of the one who had herself flayed just to gain the fresher complexion of a new skin? . . . I have seen some of them swallow sand and ashes, and work deliberately to ruin their stomach, so as to get pale complexions. To get a slim body, Spanish style, what torture do they not endure, tight-laced and braced, until they suffer great gashes in their sides, right to the live flesh—yes, sometimes even until they die of it?

As for those who can't be too rich, in the same essay Montaigne goes back another fifteen hundred years and quotes the Roman philosopher Seneca: "They are poor in the midst of riches, which is the worst kind of poverty."

Think of Imelda Marcos and her 4,600 pairs of shoes. Even more of the tight-lipped, hard-driven executive who will not take a full weekend with his family for fear of being edged out of a deal. "We go on ever fattening this pile," Montaigne concludes, "increasing it with one sum after another, until we deprive ourselves sordidly of the enjoyment of our own possessions and place our only joy in keeping them and not using them."

Whether it be for riches or thinness, fitness or knowledge or fame, the drive for perfection shuts out all other people and pleasures one by one. It is an addiction, like cocaine: ever more deadly in proportion to its purity.

When the Lilliputians guessed that Gulliver's watch was his god, their instincts were good. Our gods are the things we worship. Promptness, tolerance, and piety. Beauty, money, work, and power. The list could go on forever. In and of itself, none of these is a bad thing. But when we lose our perspective and transfer primary allegiance to any particular value or object, we are committing idolatry.

Leo Tolstoy is a perfect example. He so loved God that he sacrificed his only wife. Having discovered the great commandment of love as taught by Jesus—love to God and love to neighbor—he took almost everything he had, including all rights to and royalties from his books, and gave it to the poor. When his wife proved less than understanding, he wrote an eloquent novella, *The Kreutzer Sonata,* championing the practice of celibacy. Shortly thereafter Sonya Tolstoy gave birth to their thirteenth child.

She tried to understand. "Obviously nothing can be said against the assertion that it is good to be perfect," she acknowledged in a letter to her husband. "[I suppose] that it is necessary to remind people constantly that they should be perfect, and to point out to them the ways in which they can reach perfection. But I must confess I find it difficult."

I certainly wouldn't have wanted to be Tolstoy's wife. Or Carrie Nation's husband, for that matter. But genius has its own rules. Most of us are exempt from them.

Another problem with perfection is that having failed to exact it from ourselves, we continue to expect it from others, especially when they call to mind our own faults and foibles. Nothing is harder to tolerate than one's own weakness mirrored in another, especially someone dear to us.

You have decided to cut down on watching television. Not a bad decision. But now every time your spouse or roommate turns on the television, you lapse into a simmering rage. Things such as this can become an obsession. When others fail to cooperate in our virtuous ventures we respond with a vengeance. Yet vengeance is never a virtue. Neither are unkindness, insensitivity, or sanctimoniousness.

In the gospels there is a story about a man possessed of a demon. Once cast out, it passes through waterless places, seeking rest but finding none. And so it decides, "I will return to my house from which I came." When the spirit arrives home, it finds its erstwhile house empty and inviting. So what does it do but go straight out and find seven friends, each more evil than the last. They, in turn, without even a blink of the master's eye, enter and dwell there, "and the last state of that man becomes worse than the first" (Matt. 12:43–45).

The story is familiar to most of us. We vow to cast some demon from our lives, attack it with vigor and determination, and drive it away. But we forget one thing: it is not the only demon in the world. And when it comes to demons, especially those we have no eye for when they enter, there is nothing more inviting than a spanking-clean house.

If perfectionism is dangerous, it is also joyless. In Milton's hell, Satan bears all the burdens of the world and none of its joys. As are so many of us, he is trapped, living in the two dimensions that distinguish time from eternity—past and future—obsessing on his fall from glory and his dream of revenge.

This is the principal difference between fallen and unfallen angels. Unfallen angels may perhaps be less brilliant, but certainly no less bright; for they are not in the least bit driven to possess what is not theirs to have, only ambitious for what they can savor here and now. Freed from nostalgia and from longing, unfallen angels are witnesses to joy.

Our religion could benefit from a bit more of this. Most religion, rife with perfectionism, with nostalgia for some lost arcadia and a longing for some future paradise, squeezes the present out, confounding eternity with something that is not ours today but *someday* will be ours, if only we will purge ourselves according to its arch specifications. Grave, forbidding, and solemn, born of fear and inspiring fear, otherworldly and antiworldly, lacking a gift for play and laughter, such religion smacks far more of the demonic than it does of the celestial.

To sacrifice solemnity doesn't mean to sacrifice seriousness. We can have a serious conversation with our children without intimidating them by the gravity of our demeanor. Certainly we are often serious when we play, which doesn't imply that we are not having a good time. We are serious when we write a love letter. And nothing could be more serious than to watch the sun dance on the water's edge, a perfect conjunction of the four elements, earth, air, water, and fire.

Religious solemnity is mock-seriousness. We act the way

we think we ought to act when worshiping God. As if gravity were a sacrament, and laughter a sin.

Most hardboiled skeptics fare no better. Applying the sharp but tiny scalpel of rationalism, they first strip the creation of its mystery and then, like the philosophical taxidermists they are, stuff it into a tight skin of their own narrow devising. They are a bit like the boy who wanted to get a better understanding of butterflies. He killed one, pinned it to a board, and then announced triumphantly after a week of careful observation that butterflies cannot fly.

As for the substitutes for religion that atheists and determinists seem driven to fashion for themselves according to the principles of science or human behavior as they perceive it, these too are nothing if not solemn. Whether manifested in the arcadian utopias of nineteenth-century "free-thinkers," or in the futuristic determinism of contemporary Marxist states, after freedom, humor is almost always the next thing to go. Apparently, it is as treasonous for us to poke fun at our own creations as it is blasphemous for God's children to enjoy themselves when worshiping God.

Jesus said that unless we become like little children we cannot enter the realm of heaven. Just observe a child in unself-conscious play. Or, for that matter—though they are harder to find these days—a sage walking through the woods. When his religious contemporaries knitted their brows and preached that "Miracles have ceased," Ralph Waldo Emerson smiled to himself and in his journal wrote, "Have they, indeed? When? They had not ceased this afternoon when I walked into the wood and got into bright, miraculous sunshine, in shelter from the roaring wind." Fail to look upon the world with the wide eyes of a child or sage, and we too will entertain angels unawares.

In his book *A Rumor of Angels,* Peter Berger speaks of "the comic relief of redemption; it makes it possible for us to laugh and to play with a new fullness. This in no way implies a remoteness from the moral challenges of the moment, but rather the most careful attention to each human gesture that we encounter or that we may be called upon to perform in the affairs of the world." Nothing could be more serious. When, playing a game perhaps, or making love, or in any act of unself-conscious giving, we lose ourselves in the moment, past and future disappear and we step into a new dimension, one awash with angels, the eternal now, bringing with it, in Berger's words, "a beatific immunity" to pain and death.

Remember, angels are both God's messengers and God's message, witnesses to eternity in time, to the presence of the divine amidst the ordinary. Every moment of every day is riddled by their traces.

Real angels are not dull. They don't wear halos and strum harps and sing the same old song over and over again forever. In fact, every song an angel sings is a new song, every note a new note, just as every moment of our lives is a new moment, another opportunity for awakening, for the gift and receipt of grace.

Neither are angels incorporeal. They are ideas of God, and every one of God's ideas is expressed in God's creation. Angels are sweet and sour and salty, wet and dry, hard and soft, sharp and smooth. They fly, yes, but in flights of our own fancy. To awaken to their presence, we too must learn to fly, let our imaginations soar, awaken from dreams of yesterday and tomorrow where death and perfection abide, to the living dream that is ours today.

The angels do have two useful tricks to help us with

this. The first they call "nostalgia for the present." Nostalgia is a form of sentimentality focusing on the past. We conjure up images of life as it once was, or as we wish to remember it, and pine away for the good old days. This is a highly selective process. Certain memories are distilled and embellished upon. The result is a kind of fantasy, purified of imperfections, even of reality. We long for what never really was, regret its passing, and rue the present for its absence.

But with nostalgia for the present, today is the good old day. We look wistfully at that which is ours this very instant to savor and to save. As Marcus Aurelius wrote in his meditations, "Do not indulge in dreams of having what you have not, but reckon up the chief of the blessings you do possess and then thankfully remember how you would crave for them if they were not yours."

Another angelic trick treats the future exactly as nostalgia for the present does the past. The angels call it "looking forward to the present." Take something you already have and then imagine you want it. More than anything else in the world. For nothing is so sweet as that which we want when we have it.

To get the most out of each, the angels would probably tell you to practice both at once. Imagine that today was tomorrow, and also yesterday. Then, instead of pining over a past that is no more or longing for a future that may never be, we are freed to greet the present with a wistful and anticipatory welcome.

This has nothing to do with living *for* today, in wanton disregard for consequences that might follow upon self-indulgent or thoughtless behavior. Rather, it is a matter of living *in* today, being fully present, awake and alive.

"It is a passion beyond all possessiveness," writes Peter Marin in *Harper's* magazine, a fierce love of the world and a fierce joy in the transience of things made beautiful by their impermanence. I would not trade this day for heaven, no matter what name we call it by. Or rather, I think that if there is a heaven, it is something like this, a pleasure taken in life, this gift of one's comrades at rest momentarily under the trees, and the taste of satisfaction, and the promise of grace, alive in one's hands and mouth.

Last winter, sailing south on a beautiful ship, I awakened early one morning and went out on deck. The salt air was brisk, the sky a canopy of clouds. One other passenger was standing by the rail. "Lousy day," he said. "Not great," I replied.

And then a deckhand carrying a bucket and mop, an old man with a bright red face and a cockney accent, came down the stairway singing at the top of his lungs. A rousing, slightly off-color ballad it was, and my fellow passenger took great offense. What offended him was not the song so much as the singer. "Hasn't the bloke got eyes?" he muttered, and then, confronting him directly said, "What do you sing on a good day, a dirge?"

"A good day? Why, this is a good day."

"You've got to be kidding. I paid a lot of money for this, and what do I get? I might as well have stayed home."

"Guv'ner," the old man replied, a twinkle in his eye, "there's many a blind man who would give his eyeteeth to look out on this day."

Change it about and what Barthelme said does turn out to be true. It is a curiosity of writing about human beings that, sometimes at least, one turns out to be writing about angels.

3. On the Side of the Angels

Good kings who disembowelled for a tax,
Good popes who brought all good to jeopardy,
Good Christians who sat still in easy chairs
And damned the general world for standing up—
Now may the good God pardon all good men.

ELIZABETH BARRETT BROWNING

"Do you have any doubts that you are right?"
"None whatsoever."
"Never?"
"Not once. I've been a Christian for 28 years."

THE REV. JERRY FALWELL

If angels had nothing better to do, which it turns out is never the case, I am sure they would enjoy pondering the results of public opinion surveys. For instance, this recent poll sponsored by *People* magazine. Prompted by the question "If people enjoy watching fictional misbehavior, how do they feel about it in real life," a thousand readers shared their own feelings about the Ten Commandments, the seven deadly sins, and sin in general. For those blessed with an ironic temperament, the results are quite illuminating.

According to the survey, the most difficult of the Ten Commandments for most of us to keep is "Thou shalt not take the name of the Lord thy God in vain." The problem here is swearing, I suppose, though that is scarcely what God had in mind when he delivered the law to Moses. Save for "Thou shalt not kill," we seem to think that the easiest commandment is "Thou shalt have no other Gods before me." I would have put that one first, not next to last. The gods we worship are many—success, beauty, money, work, sex, drugs, television, fame—each with its own cadre of principalities and powers to keep us from noticing how often and how readily we lapse into idolatry.

Readers then were asked to list as many of the seven deadly sins as they could. Half of the respondents couldn't name any of them. I wonder, do these people sleep any better at night than the rest of us?

Topping the list of "known" deadly sins was avarice, followed closely by lust and envy, with sloth and gluttony as also-rans. Pride and anger came in last, which surely says something about what Santayana once described as "the native good will, complacency, thoughtlessness, and optimism" of Americans.

The most fascinating part of the survey is "*People* Magazine's Sindex: A Reader's Guide to Misbehavior." Fifty-one activities are listed, and respondents registered on a scale of 1 to 10 how bad they would feel if they were to engage in any of them. Some of the rankings are a little puzzling. For instance, spouse-swapping edges out adultery, which suggests that we consider it slightly worse to sin with our spouse's connivance than we do without it. Dropping down the scale, selfishness and laziness are each considered much more serious lapses than not voting. I should have thought that not voting was emblematic of both. Most telling of all, though murder is clearly tops on our index of sins, capital punishment scores far lower than atheism, parking in a handicapped zone, cutting into line, and idle gossip.

One problem with being on the side of the angels is that we first have to figure out which side the angels are on. Do they keep score when we cut into line or gossip on the phone, and yet turn their heads when we sentence a fellow human being to death?

To compound our dilemma, if taken literally the Bible is of little help to us here. The sixth commandment clearly says, "Thou shalt not kill," but there is ample evidence throughout the scriptures that God has a selective habit of looking the other way when the right people break his rules.

Take the story of Abraham in Egypt (Gen. 12:10–20). There is a famine in Israel, so Abram (as he was known back then) and his wife Sarah seek respite by journeying south. When they arrive in Egypt, Abram is worried for his safety, but he has a plan to ensure that he will come to no harm. He says to his wife, "Sarah, you are a beautiful woman. When the Egyptians see you, they will say, 'Let's get rid of her husband so that we can have her for ourselves.' I know you love me, Sarah, and would not want me to come to any harm. All you have to do is say that you're my sister, and everything will be fine." For Abram, that is.

Don't expect to find a ready moral here, certainly not one that you could easily explain to your children. For, like a "good" wife, Sarah does precisely what she is told. Because of her great beauty, she comes to the attention of the pharaoh. In all innocence, he invites her to move in with him, which she does. This isn't exactly wife-swapping, because pharaoh remains in the dark about what he is actually doing, though Abram does receive a handsome bounty in exchange for Sarah. As a token of his appreciation, the pharaoh lavishes upon Abram sheep and oxen and he-asses and menservants and maidservants and she-asses and camels. What more could a man possibly want?

When all of this happens, God understandably is furious. But not at Abram. God takes his anger out on poor pharaoh, sending down a plague upon him and his house. Finally, upon learning the truth about Sarah and accordingly the cause for his distress, the pharaoh calls Abram to him. "What in the world have you done to me?" he asks. "Why didn't you tell me in the first place that Sarah was your wife, and not your sister?" Pharaoh sends them both packing, but "Abram was very rich," the Bible reminds us, "in cattle, in silver and in gold."

One more story, also from Genesis (27:1–40). Abraham's son, Isaac, lies aged and dying. He sends for his eldest child, Esau, requesting that Esau bring him venison, in response to which Isaac will give him his blessing and with it his due inheritance as firstborn son. But when Esau's mother, Rebekah, overhears this, she begins to scheme on behalf of Jacob, Esau's brother and Rebekah's favorite.

Isaac was blind, but as you may recall Esau was "a hairy man" and Jacob "a smooth man," which meant that Isaac should have no trouble telling the two apart. To overcome this stumbling block to perfidy, Rebekah has a remedy. She outfits Jacob's neck and hands with goat skins. So disguised, while Esau is out hunting to bring a savory gift to his father, Jacob presents himself at Isaac's bedside.

"I am Esau, thy firstborn," Jacob says. "I have done as you asked. Arise and eat of my venison, that thy soul may bless me."

"How is it you have found it so quickly, my son?"

"Because the Lord thy God brought it to me," Jacob replies.

"Come near, that I may feel you, my son, to be sure that you are my very son, Esau, or not." Jacob approaches his father. "The voice is Jacob's voice," Isaac says, "but the hands are the hands of Esau. Art thou my very son, Esau?"

"Yes, Father, I am," Jacob lies again. And so Isaac blesses him.

Between these two stories, at least five of the ten commandments are broken. "Thou shalt not take the name of the Lord thy God in vain"; "Honor thy father"; "Thou shalt not bear false witness"; "Thou shalt not commit [or cause to commit] adultery"; and "Thou shalt not steal." In fact, in Abram's case you could even throw in the one about not coveting your neighbor's "manservant, nor his maidservant, nor his ox, etc." So who is on the side of the angels here? The pharaoh and Esau, or Abram and Jacob? Evidently, it is sometimes far more prudent to forget about being on the side of the angels, so long as you make sure that the angels are on *your* side.

But such would be to mistake the Bible for what it is not, the ultimate in cookbooks. As my colleague John Buehrens pans this approach: "You want to find out what to do about your adolescent child. Just consult Proverbs 13:1" ("A wise son hears his father's instruction, but a scoffer does not listen to rebuke").

As little as they might wish to admit it, when it comes to the Bible fundamentalists of the right and the left make the very same mistake. Both are captive to abject literalism. One group enshrines every word of the Bible as divine, the absolute and only word of God. The other, resting its conclusions on no less exacting a criterion, rejects every jot and tittle precisely because the Bible turns out *not* to be inerrant.

One thing we simply can't seem to tolerate is ambiguity. We want things sharp and clean, yes or no, nothing gray. To convince ourselves that we are right, we demonstrate that others are wrong. So what? Of course they are, to one extent or another; but so are we.

And that is the most refreshing thing about the Bible. The Bible is about sinners sinning and still being saved. It is full of surprises designed to awaken us from our smugness: human laws preempted by divine law, primogeniture cast by the wayside, parties thrown for prodigal sons, whores having precedence in the Kingdom over moguls. If we had as good a sense of humor as the angels do, we would read the Bible and have a good long laugh at ourselves.

As did the angel who was supposed to be presiding over a pool down by the sheep-gate in Jerusalem. Legend had it that this angel, whenever the surface of the waters moved, would heal the first person to jump in of whatever ailed him. A lame man had lain by the pool for thirty-eight years, waiting for his chance. Finally Jesus came by one Sabbath day. The waters were not moving, but he said to him anyway, "Take up your pallet and walk." And so the man did. At which point the same authorities who believed in the angel exploded in anger—not only at the man, for breaking the Sabbath commandment by porting his bed about on Sabbath day, but also at Jesus, for inciting him to do so (John 5:2–18).

You don't believe the story about the man at the well? You didn't see it with your own two eyes? It offends the laws of nature? I don't know about you, but I have seen people languish for thirty-eight years without ever doing a single thing about their plight. They were offered a hundred sure-fire cures by their friends—psychotherapy, rolfing, a macrobiotic diet—but still lay by the wellside waiting for an angel to come by. And then one day, something happened.

Someone came by and said, "I'm not going to help you, do it yourself." And that was that.

In short, there is no "correct" way to read the Bible. It is important to remember this, because most of those who consider themselves to be on the side of the angels use such things as Bibles to justify doing what by any other measure would surely be judged wrong.

Let's go back for a moment to the Sindex. It wasn't listed, but I wonder how nuclear war would have ranked? High, I should hope, perhaps somewhere between child abuse and suicide, for surely it is both. More telling would be an item on increasing the Pentagon's budget to augment our nuclear arsenals. If capital punishment can be listed as a sin, certainly the arms buildup should qualify. Had it appeared, even judging from the voting patterns of those who believe that not to vote is bad, my guess is that it would rank rather low on our list of sins, say, between "calling in sick when you're not" and overeating.

This is worth pondering, because one of the ways we justify our arms buildup is by quoting the Bible. Not only is nuclear preparedness high on the Christian agenda of the New Religious Right, but to justify an ever-escalating arms race scripture is cited even by the highest officials in government. In fact, allusions to the Soviet Union as "the Evil Empire" are plucked straight from the Book of Revelation, the proof-text for Armageddon.

Given the stakes, questions about whose side the angels are on are not entirely frivolous. To begin with, how can we be sure that the angels are watching over *us?* According to John Cardinal Wright, we can take comfort from the fact that even in the Soviet Union, "Monuments to the angel's influence among us abound everywhere. In Moscow, merging into the skyline of the Kremlin rises the dome of the Cathedral of the Archangel, within which is still venerated, however covertly, its precious icon of Saint Michael the Warrior"—the very angel whom Henry Adams once described as standing "for Church and State, and both militant." But which church and which state? Do the Russians who offer up their prayers to Saint Michael pray that he will rescue them from Soviet thralldom, or do they pray for him to deliver them from the threat of U.S. militarism? Probably both, but it might be prudent for those who believe in Michael's much-vaunted first-strike capability to pray in return that he is not listening.

It is a sad commentary on the potential abuses of religion, but judging from history, next to "in vain," and during periods of personal tribulation, the name of God is most likely to be invoked with true passion by old men sending young men to war—the sword in one hand and the scriptures in the other, "Onward Christian Soldiers" with Jesus as the linchpin. In fact, from the beginning of recorded history, more blood has been spilled under "God's" banner than any other.

The Crusades are far from being over. Protestants and Catholics in Ireland. Sikhs and Hindus in India. Jews and Moslems in the Middle East. Christians and Communists almost everywhere else.

It's not that war cannot be justified, though given the almost inevitable consequence of geocide, nuclear war is a different matter entirely. Our question here must be this: Do the angels pick sides, and if so, how do we know that the side they pick is ours?

From the *Iliad* on, stories abound of gods and angels swooping down from on high to join in mortals' combat.

And not only as a literary device, as with Milton's "airy knights" or Shakespeare's "fierce fiery warriors." In World War II, the Air Chief Marshall of Great Britain actually believed that in the battle for Britain, angels filled the cockpits of dead pilots and helped to ensure the victory. Even more famous is this tale from World War I, "The Angels of Mons."

The story first ran in the London *Evening News* on September 14, 1915, under British author Arthur Machen's byline. An apparition of "shining" phantom bowmen from the field of Agincourt had apparently covered the British infantrymen during their bloody retreat from Mons. Machen quoted one officer's testimony as follows. "On the night of the 27th I was riding along the column with two other officers. . . . As we rode along I became conscious of the fact that in the fields on both sides of the road along which we were marching I could see a very large body of horsemen." The spectral bowmen let fly of their arrows and German soldiers were mowed down by the score.

Shortly thereafter, several confirmations of the same vision were reported. In the book *On the Side of the Angels,* published later that same year, Harold Begbie quoted a dying German prisoner of war who confessed to a German reluctance to attack, "because of the thousands of troops behind us." British soldiers said they had seen an apparition of Saint George; French soldiers, Saint Michael. One wounded lance corporal told a reporter that he had seen three shining figures in the sky in a vision that lasted thirty-five minutes. There was only one problem with all of this. As Machen confessed later, he had made the whole thing up.

The moment anyone reports that the angels are with us,

it seems that we will go to any length, straining all credulity, to believe this is the case. Especially when the angels are armed. But scour the horizon as we may, the only angels who are likely to materialize will turn out to be apparitions.

Not that there were no angels bearing witness in World War I. The young British poet Wilfred Owen (who was later killed in the war) inverts the story of Abraham and Isaac, turning it into a contemporary parable. Convinced that he is acting according to God's will, Abraham binds his son, builds parapets and trenches, and stretches forth his hand for the kill.

> When lo! an angel called him out of heav'n
> Saying, Lay not thy hand upon the lad,
> Neither do anything to him. Behold,
> A ram, caught in a thicket by its horns;
> Offer the Ram of Pride instead of him.
> But the old man would not so, but slew his son,
> And half the seed of Europe, one by one.

The same lesson pertains in interpersonal as well as international relations. It is as if the angels were trying to remind us: *When you do act, act with determination, but never cease to beware the motives for and potential consequences of even your best-intentioned actions. Above all else, do not presume that things will work out as you think they should, or should work out as you think they ought.*

If there is such a thing as ultimate forgiveness, I should wager that it is offered for everything but pride.

Especially when it comes to making war, we must be careful before presuming upon God's preferences. But even here, there is at least some evidence as to the direction in which we should err. Find the grain and cut against it.

Thoreau. Gandhi. Martin Luther King, Jr. The testimony of prophets, often offered at great personal cost, almost always defies contemporary assumptions and disregards questions of expediency.

When Abraham Lincoln, in embarking upon war to reunite the Union, was assured that God was on his side, he responded that this really wasn't the issue. What we should ask ourselves instead is whether we are on the side of God. And that is a very different thing indeed.

To begin with, we can never be sure. This does not impede our taking action, only qualifies the actions we do take with a touch of prudent humility. One good rule of thumb is to be most mistrustful of those who are quickest to claim divine connivance in their cause. Another—though, sadly, it is not always possible to act without violence—is to remember that angels, by definition if not popular depiction, are never armed.

There is a very good reason for this. Of nonviolent resistance to evil, Mohandas Gandhi said:

If this kind of force is used in a cause that is unjust, only the person using it suffers. He does not make others suffer for his mistakes. Men have before now done many things which were subsequently found to have been wrong. No man can claim that he is absolutely in the right or that a particular thing is wrong because he thinks so, but it is wrong for him so long as that is his deliberate judgment.

Which means that we act, but always in such a way that if we prove later to have been wrong, our error is compounded as little as possible by the nature of our action.

None of us can sustain this. We perform little acts of cruelty and violence every day we live. All of us do. An unkind word, or thought, or deed. The gratuitous violence that always follows upon self-absorption, whether grounded in anger, envy, avarice, lust, gluttony, sloth, or pride.

But sometimes, more often by accident than design, we lose ourselves and angels find us. We empty ourselves and angels fill us up. Angels knock upon our door and we open it. And, not knowing who or precisely what it is that we are welcoming, we welcome them in. Flanked in the doorway, we gaze out upon the creation, with reverence for all life, knowing that when others suffer we suffer too, for we are part of one body, the body of God.

And then we too are on the side of the angels.

4. Angels and Strangers

Can anything good come out of Nazareth?

JOHN 1:46

In 1971, years before we had children, Amy and I sailed around the world on an oil tanker. Her name was *Pathfinder* and she was a supertanker, built specifically to fit the Panama Canal. Back then, before the shift in oil fortunes, she was a world-class money maker. Her only passengers, we were ensconced in the owner's quarters courtesy of Amy's father, Gordon Furth, who then was executive vice president of a mining and shipping company. We were like pilot fish, tiny, colorful human hangers on, just along for the ride and for the pleasurable company of all those books, carefully packed in four of our five bags, texts we had been assigned but had not read during our undergraduate years at Stanford.

We had heard of people who spent their summers on assignment for the Forest Service as fire watchers living all alone above the treetops in Robinson Crusoe houses. This was a little like that. Every night we watched the sea catch fire as the sun went down. Sailing from Portland, Maine, to El Segundo, California, around the horn of Africa and through the Straits of Singapore, we spent sixty-three days on water and ten long hours on land. Our friends thought we were crazy.

One of the most interesting things about this ship was its social and political structure. In charge was the captain, an amiable American, with whom we had little else in common. Second in rank was the chief engineer. He was German, and a fairly good chess player. The four of us had large forward cabins. We ate dinner together every night in the Captain's dining room. Everyone else on the crew, from the officers down to the lowly purser who waited table for us, was Japanese. They slept in tiny cabins or dormitories aft.

Morito San, a man in his mid-forties, was the purser. He cleaned our cabin, brought us lunch, kept me supplied with Scotch, and did the cooking—hearty American fare to suit the captain's taste. He even baked his first cake for Amy on her birthday. The captain, by his demeanor as much as by instruction, discouraged us from fraternizing with Morito San, the one crew member who spoke fairly good English. Because of his station, we were led to understand not only that familiarity would be inappropriate, but that Morito San himself would find it painful.

Two days before we reached home port, Morito San came into our cabin and asked us if we would mind terribly if he took a few moments of our time. He had noticed that we were reading Thomas Mann. He told us a story about how he had walked the streets of Tokyo all night long with tears welling in his eyes upon finishing *The Magic Mountain* for the first time. He said the reason that he came to sea was to have uninterrupted time for reading and study. And also for his poetry. We asked Morito San about his poetry. He ran back to his room and produced a handsome volume of ancient Japanese haiku. He sat with us and shared in simple, elegant words the principles of haiku. And then he wrote us a poem.

As it turns out, Morito San also read Plato. One of Plato's most memorable images is his metaphor of the cave from *The Republic*. We are sitting facing a wall, with our legs and necks chained so that we cannot turn and see what is going on behind us. Through the opening of the cave, the light shines. Between us and it there is a ramp along which figures walk, carrying vessels and statues. Their images play in shadow form on the wall of the cave.

What would happen, Socrates asks, if we were to be freed from our bondage and invited to leave our prison and walk toward the light? At first we would be blinded, but even once our eyes became accustomed to the brightness, if an instructor were to point out the figures and objects along the ramp and name them for us, would we recognize them?

Socrates suggests that initially we would not, for they would be far less familiar to us than the shadows they cast. And if we *were* finally enlightened as to the true nature of things and then returned to share our new knowledge with our fellow prisoners, those who had never moved out of their den, they would surely shake their heads and say that we had returned from up above "without our eyes; and that it was better not even to think of ascending; and if any one tried to loose another and lead him up to the light, let them only catch the offender, and they would put him to death."

Each of these stories is about appearances and reality. We are under tremendous pressure to conform to the mores, opinions, practices, and prejudices of our time, whatever they may be. Often, we do so without question, because we know no better. We too see more clearly in the dark than in the light. And if challenged, we tend to resist, defending our prejudices, for change is painful and its results unpredictable. Pull one thread and the whole garment might unravel.

Though angels are both the messengers and the message of God, that makes them no easier to receive. For one thing, we almost never recognize them, even when they knock at our door. I said at the outset that if angels came wrapped in packages we would almost always pick the wrong one. We would pick the big one or the one wrapped in silver foil with a fancy blue bow, certainly not the one in brown paper fastened with a string.

Angels are goodness in disguise. They almost always wear masks. As messages of God, they are hidden. As messengers, they are strangers.

Remember the three strangers who appeared to Abraham on the plain of Mamre. He invited them in, had water fetched to wash their feet, and suggested they rest under a shade tree, comforting their hearts before moving on. Sarah fixed them a fine meal of fresh bread and butter, milk, and veal. Abraham set it before them and stood by as they feasted under the tree. At which point they announced that Sarah, already an old woman, would give birth to a son. She laughed. What she forgot was that she was entertaining angels. They left, and all that was promised came to pass (Gen. 18:1–15).

If angels are strangers, how can we recognize them? Often we can't, which is why it is wise to do as Abraham and Sarah did and offer hospitality to strangers who may pass our way. Strangers like the little gray old man in the fairy tale who asks for bread, the one who holds wishes in his power, even the gift of life and death. Strangers like Jesus, who in Martin Luther's words, "conducted himself so humbly and associated with sinful men and women, and as a consequence was not held in great esteem," on account of which "the devil overlooked him and did not recognize him. For the devil is farsighted; he looks only for what is big and high and attaches himself to that; he does not look at that which is low down and beneath himself."

For this, a single illustration. People with AIDS.

I grew up with a glib and thoughtless prejudice against homosexuals. Perhaps all prejudice, reinforced by stereotypes and based upon ignorance and fear, is glib and thoughtless. Mine certainly was. It was not until my first year in seminary when my closest friend turned out to be gay that the shutters were lifted from my eyes.

For most of us, our sexual preferences and practices are far from being the most important distinguishing feature of our being. If I were asked for adjectives to describe myself, heterosexual would fall close to the end of the list. The things we share tend to be universal. We may not share color or faith or sexual preference, but we do share birth, pain, passion, love, fear, and death.

When we forget this, we need awakening. And those who most surely can awaken us are the very people we are readiest to reject, the ones flanked by angels.

Three years ago I officiated at my first AIDS-related funeral. I counseled the young man's mother, a woman from Australia who discovered that her son was gay at the same time that she discovered he was dying. I think I was of some small help, but I failed then to recognize that this was not an isolated instance, but rather a pattern of human suffering that demanded more than a personal response.

Historically, the church has seized upon epidemics and plagues as a sign of God's displeasure. I think it was Seventeenth-century Puritan and Calvinist Cotton Mather who said, "Sickness is in fact the whip of God for the sins of many." This general assessment is compounded by the need to find a scapegoat.

In the fourteenth century, at the time of the bubonic

plague in Europe, tens of thousands of Jews were slaughtered, their shops looted, their homes burned. By 1351, when the plague finally subsided, scarcely a Jew remained alive in Germany or the Low Countries.

Both factors are combined in a sermon delivered by the local priest in Albert Camus's novel *The Plague*. Here is Father Paneloux's theological assessment of the plague's visitation upon his own town:

Calamity has come to you, my brethren, and, my brethren, you deserved it. . . . The first time this scourge appears in history, it was wielded to strike down the enemies of God. Pharaoh set himself up against the divine will, and the plague beat him to his knees. Thus from the dawn of recorded history the scourge of God has humbled the proud of heart and laid low those who hardened themselves against Him. . . . If today the plague is in your midst, that is because the hour has struck for taking thought. The just man need have no fear, but the evildoer has good cause to tremble. For plague is the flail of God and the world His threshing-floor, and implacably He will thresh out His harvest until the wheat is separated from the chaff.

This sort of thinking is not out of date. Jerry Falwell and others expressly link the AIDS epidemic to God's displeasure with homosexuals and intravenous drug users. I am surprised that they leave out the Haitians.

I believe in a different God than Jerry Falwell does. I believe in a God who inspired Jesus to reach out to the poor and the dispossessed, to prostitutes and prodigal children, to humble folk and outcasts. Not only to reach out to them, but to hold them in special esteem.

One of Camus's characters asks the protagonist, Dr. Rieux, " 'What did you think of Paneloux's sermon, doctor?' The question was asked in a quite ordinary tone, and Rieux answered in the same tone. 'I've seen too much of hospitals to relish any idea of collective punishment.' "

There is a difference, of course, between AIDS and the bubonic plague. But as with the plague, the revenge here is not God's, any more than it is God who exacts revenge by casting to her death a child who is playing carelessly in an open third-story window.

Think of the problem of children with AIDS and the public schools. My own children, Nina and Twig, are in the public schools of New York City, and I deeply believe that due caution should be exercised, especially by the parents of children with AIDS who may be vulnerable to infection. But if children with AIDS are denied a place in the schools it will be the first time in history that a medical quarantine has been established on a group—in this case school-age children—before a single known case of transmission from a member of that group has been recorded.

Proportionately, for every parent who is willing to keep his or her child away from a school in which an AIDS patient is enrolled, there should be hundreds of parents organizing a campaign to demand signed release forms ensuring that every time their child travels in a neighbor's car the seat belts are fastened.

Fear kills our ability to love, because it throws up walls. Apart from what this does to others, think about ourselves. When we hide behind our fears, not daring to come out, building our walls higher and higher, finally we are imprisoned in our own protected little garden. Even this we cannot enjoy, because the sun is blocked out and our souls, like plants, wither and die.

Another thing about plants—the more you give away their flowers, the stronger grow their roots. When we are afraid, and therefore without love, we have no one to give away our flowers to. There is such a thing as hell on earth. For the most part, it is populated by people who fear so deeply that they cannot love. One of the reasons I believe in hell is that I have seen so many closed gardens.

I was on a talk show recently, and a woman called in to say she had heard that All Souls Church had established an AIDS task force. She wanted to know how I, as a religious leader, could have failed to heed the biblical injunction against homosexuality. I wish I could report that I parried her thrust in the way that it ought to have been. Instead I said something about the religious imperative to respond to those who are suffering with as much love as we can muster.

But that's not the answer. Not to her question, anyway. If I were a biblical literalist, not only would I be speaking out against homosexuality, but also in favor of slavery, the subjugation of women, and even, if some passages of the Bible are to be credited, polygamy.

But I have more respect for the scriptures than that. What inspires me in the Bible is not the letter but the spirit. If you read the prophets and the gospels carefully, with certain exceptions one message resounds time and again. God is not on the side of the persecutors but on the side of the persecuted. The realm of heaven is revealed not at the banquet of the rich, but in the crumbs of the poor. Jesus of all people would far rather celebrate the humanity of a little one than the power of the ruling class.

We may know little about ourselves, but our ignorance of others is astounding. Which means that the surest way to grow in wisdom is through our acquaintance with others, especially others markedly different from us. In this case, I can think of almost no exceptions. Take someone distinctive and he or she will have something to teach us. No amount of hobnobbing with those who share our preferences and prejudices will accomplish as much.

Distinctive is a good word. It means special, unique, telling in some important way. And so if we are looking for God's traces, we would be wise to begin with a persecuted minority. If the Bible has anything to teach us, it is that the persecuted are especially beloved by God. They are blessed, and we in turn are blessed by them. Every minority, every oppressed group, every distinctive individual excluded by the prevailing mores and fashions of the times, is one of God's most precious children, a special agent of God on earth.

It is easy to love those who resemble us. But if I read the scriptures right, in God's eye such love, if essential, is not sufficient. God's challenge is to love those who are different and learn from them. Male and female. Black, brown, red, yellow, and white. Christian, Moslem, Buddhist, Hindu, Jew, agnostic, atheist. Straight and gay.

None of these distinctions matter all that much. Not in God's eye, not in the eye of eternity. What matters is how we move from who we are to who we might be. We begin limited by race and sex and sexual preference and nationality and economic status. The sad thing is that this is also how we may end, known according to the accidents of our birth rather than the measure of our growth. Angels intervene to help us grow.

I have no interest in being gay. That's not the issue, for I have no aptitude for being gay. For me, gayness is a moot point. What I do have an aptitude for is growing beyond the provincial human territory into which I was born. I can visit other human lands, awaken to the beauty of difference, rejoice in dissimilarity, become more secure in my own distinctiveness and less threatened by the distinctiveness of others.

People with AIDS are not angels. They are human beings just like the rest of us, mortal, limited, and flawed. But if we are looking for angels, one place we are certain to find them is by the bedside of God's children when they are dying. Especially these children. As Mother Teresa reminds us, "Each one of them is Jesus in a distressing disguise."

And what did Jesus say to the man who wanted to know what example he must follow to enter the Kingdom?

> I was hungry, and you gave me to eat;
> I was naked, and you covered me;
> I was thirsty, and you gave me to drink;
> I was sick, and you visited me;
> I was a stranger, and you took me in;
> I was in prison and you came to me. . . .
> Inasmuch as you do the same
> unto one of the least of these my brethren,
> you have done it unto me. (Matt. 25:35–40)

In other words, when someone is suffering, try washing his feet. Nurture and comfort him. Go aft.

5. The Angel of Death

Life is so generous a giver, but we,
Judging its gifts by their covering,
Cast them away as ugly, or heavy, or hard.
Remove the covering, and you will find beneath it.
A living splendor, woven of love, by wisdom, with power.
Welcome it, grasp it, and you touch the
Angel's hand that brings it to you.
Everything we call a trial, a sorrow, or a duty,
Believe me, that Angel's hand is there.

FRA GIOVANNI

All God's angels come to us disguised;
Sorrow and sickness, poverty and death,
One after another lift their frowning masks,
And we behold the Seraph's face beneath,
All radiant with the glory and the calm
Of having looked upon the front of God.

JAMES RUSSELL LOWELL

Do you remember the old game Snakes and Ladders? It's
Chutes and Ladders these days, slightly domesticated but
the same game, a board game with 100 squares numbered
from bottom to top. Throwing the dice, players work their
way up rank by rank until one of them gets to the top,
thereby winning the game. The twist is that certain squares
are marked by ladders, others by snakes. You may be ever
so far behind, hit a tall ladder, and catapult into the lead.
On the other hand—and this is how I, somewhat perversely, remember the game—you may open up a terrific
lead, twenty squares ahead of your closest opposition. There
you are on square 84, 16 squares to go, victory within your

grasp, and what do you do? You throw a 9. Square 93. Unbelievable. The longest and nastiest snake on the board.

In our lives too, failure and success come within a hairsbreadth of one another. We are secure in neither. Cinderella goes to the ball and marries the prince. Richard Cory goes home one night and puts a bullet through his head.

For instance, Job was a righteous man, honest, obedient, never one to scorn his God, hardworking, faithful in every way. Yet, one by one his children were taken from him, then his fortune, then his wife.

Later editors of the book of Job could not stand the incongruity between Job's righteousness and the punishment meted out to him. So they added an appendix to the original book of Job. Their patchwork theology leaves a seam so artificial that it almost jumps off the page. A happy ending. For all his trouble, Job gets a new wife, new children, fourteen thousand head of cattle, six thousand camels, a thousand yoke of oxen, and as many she-asses.

Not bad.

Admittedly, this was before the theologians had discovered heaven. In early Judaism, life ended with death. Before the story was improved, Job's reward, despite his extraordinary hardship, lay in the knowledge—his own knowledge—that throughout he had remained faithful.

In contrast, when things go badly for us, how quickly we bargain for a trade. The happiness we seek lies at the top of an endless golden staircase. To get there we are tempted to try anything: cut corners; skip stairs; trample on our loved ones' feelings or leave them far behind. Somewhere near the top stood J. Paul Getty, the multimillionaire. No Job, at the end of his life he cursed his wealth and said he'd trade it all for one happy marriage.

The search for happiness is fraught with such pitfalls. Public people lament their loss of a private life; millions of unknowns dream of being famous. Beautiful people find reasons to regret their beauty; plain people, their plainness. One man suffers under the restrictions of marriage. Another mourns the emotional barrenness in a life of one-night stands. A homemaker wishes that she were as confident or as successful as her neighbor, a businesswoman. And right next door, the very woman she envies envies her, longing for the children she herself has sacrificed for a professional career. Just where you would think that the grass should be green, it is dying.

I am no longer startled by this. What startles me still is precisely the opposite. So often, where you would think that the grass would surely be dying, it is green.

A man is struggling with alcoholism. He has been forced to declare bankruptcy. Everything in his life will have to be rebuilt from the ground up, but he hasn't had a drink for two months. And he is happy.

A woman is fired from her job. She seizes the opportunity to reflect upon what really matters to her, savors the free time, goes on a long vacation, and then returns to look for work, refreshed and renewed. And she is happy.

A man is dying. He has been given a week at most to live. He and his wife lie together in their bed. They talk about old times, watch a tennis match on television, and look at family pictures. And, in a special way, they too are happy.

I spend time with such people every week. I spend time with them because they are in trouble. Hard times don't always bring out the best in people, but they can. Perhaps it is because adversity, not always but sometimes, tends to strip away our illusions. We are forced to work within tightly drawn and well-defined limits. When this happens, everything within those limits is heightened. Little things take on a much higher degree of importance. We count as blessings things that during other times we simply took for granted. The sky gets dark and the stars come out.

The angels come out too. At least it seems that angels are most likely to come out at night. During dark nights of the soul. In the shadow of death. As Ralph Waldo Emerson said, "It is in rugged crises, in unweariable endurance, and in aims which put sympathy out of the question, that the angel is shown."

It is not that angels don't come out in the daytime, when our lives are bright and all is well. They are there. We just don't notice them, for we aren't looking. When someone says we learn more from our failures than we do from our successes, or that the most important experience in his or her life was a scrape with death, or some great loss, the explanation is not that failure is to be preferred to success, or suffering to an absence of pain. This simply isn't true. But it *is* true that deep feeling and profound caring put sleepwalking to shame. Though a child or sage will be as awake to joy as she is to sorrow, most of us awaken to the beauty and fragility of life only when what we love is placed in jeopardy. Which is probably the reason that angels most often seem to come out at night.

The word happiness goes back to the root meaning "chance." It happed upon me, we say—I chanced to encounter. Most definitions of happiness, particularly popular definitions, come from one particular interpretation of this original meaning. If happiness lies in wealth or health or love, then happiness is chancy. It can come without warning and as quickly be taken away. But by another interpretation, happiness has to do with what we make of our chances. It rests in the way we respond to the things that befall us.

These two approaches are very different indeed. For instance, one person's response to illness may be to equate health with happiness. Never mind that she was not particularly happy all those years when she was healthy. Now she knows the real value of health, having lost it. Another person might respond very differently. For the first time in her entire life, she might live each day remaining to her fully, taking special pleasure in common things, savoring her time with loved ones, knowing it to be brief and therefore all the more precious.

"Ten years ago if somebody had offered me a vigorous, healthy life that would never end," Frederick Beuchner writes, "I would have said yes. Today I think I would say no. I love my life as much as I ever did and will cling on to it for as long as I can, but life without death has become as unthinkable to me as day without night or waking without sleep."

My definition of religion is a simple one. *Religion is our human response to the dual reality of being alive and having to die.* Death is not the enemy here, it is the limit that gives meaning. To embrace life for all it's worth, we must measure it against death. Only by awakening, not just to the possibilities but also to the limits of our existence, can we begin to encounter who we are by discovering how much we have to lose and how precious it is.

One Christian evangelist holds that "Death is not natural, for man was created to live and not to die." And it is true that we were immortal once, though I doubt that this is what he means. As single-celled organisms, replicated in each succeeding generation, death did not exist for us.

Having evolved into sexual beings who reproduce their kind but not themselves, life as we know it—individual, unique, and precious—depends on death. In fact, it would be impossible without death. Death is the hinge upon which our lives turn.

Among others, the Buddha recognized this. Prince Siddhartha Gautama, the man who was destined to become the Buddha, was born into royalty. His father was king of a tiny state in northeastern India. Many legends grew up surrounding Siddhartha's birth. In one his mother, Maya, was visited in a dream by a white elephant, the Indian equivalent of the Holy Spirit, who touched her side and quickened her womb. Upon hearing this, her husband called upon his wisest counselors, seeking their interpretation of her dream. They prophesied the birth of a remarkable child, one destined to be either a world ruler, or, should he choose the path of religion, a universal savior.

Like most fathers, the king was interested that his son amount to something when he grew up. Accordingly, he sought a way to guarantee the boy would choose politics over religion. The wise men told him that there was only one way to ensure this. He must shield Siddhartha from all acquaintance with old age, sickness, and death.

And so it was that Prince Siddhartha lived his youth in ignorance of the world's ills. Not only were old age, sickness, and death veiled from his sight, but every imaginable sensual delight was lavished upon him so that he would never be tempted to explore outside his bubble world and thus chance upon the harshness of reality. His father gave him three palaces, one for each season of the Indian year, and distracted him with dancing girls, jugglers, storytellers, and gaming companions. Whenever Siddhartha desired to venture into the outside world, his wish, as were all his wishes, was granted, but with this one condition. The way was carefully plotted, his route swept clean of all reminders of mortality, and the streets festooned with banners and populated with playing children and dancing youths.

One day, as usual, Siddhartha and his charioteer drove out into the world in his gilded chariot. But when they reached the country roads, his eye caught sight of something wildly at variance from anything he had ever seen before: a bent old man with a wizened face, hobbling along with a cane in his hand. "What sort of man is this, if indeed it is a man?" Siddhartha asked his driver. Not knowing how to evade the truth, his companion replied, "This is a man in old age. Once he was a babe, then a youth, and then a man in full strength and beauty. But now his strength and beauty are gone. He is withered and wasted. It is the way of life."

The next day, the specter of a sick man, prostrate, groaning, and emaciated, appeared along their route. When Siddhartha asked, "What manner of man is this?" his charioteer could only reply that each of us is prey to sickness in this life.

Finally—and despite his father's precautions it was inevitable that eventually this would happen—they came upon a funeral procession. The attendants following a corpse on a bier were weeping, tearing their clothing, and beating their breasts. Again, in response to Siddhartha's bewilderment, his companion explained, "It is death. He has been taken from those he loved, and from his home. His life is ended." The prince asked, "Are there other dead men?" To which the charioteer replied, "All who are born must die. There is no way of escape."

Such was the nature of Siddhartha's first awakening. Having come face to face with his mortality and all the suffering and illness that it entailed, he found his life—despite all its pleasures—hollow at the core, filled with diversions, empty of any consciousness of ultimate things. And so he began his pilgrimage.

The Buddha's pilgrimage led him to seek a way beyond suffering, a truth that would leave him invulnerable to life's certain pains. The Christian path is different. Through the passion of Christ, we are taught that redemption entails sacrifice. Vulnerability is the keystone of Jesus' gospel. But both teachings have this one thing in common: The beginning of enlightenment comes through an encounter with suffering and death.

We lose track of this, of course. When tragedy strikes, our tendency is to forget our natural kinship with mortality and suffering, imagining ourselves as somehow unfairly set apart, unlike all others shouldered with a unique and unbearable burden. It is hard to answer the why of death or illness with a simple because. It is hard to accept that, in the main, our loved one died because death is natural, not the exception but the rule; to admit that she contracted a rare disease because some small percentage of us simply will; to reconcile ourselves to the haphazard yet axiomatic laws that pertain to human suffering, the laws that remind us that being human we shall suffer, wrestle in the darkness, and be wounded.

As did Jacob.

Jacob was alone. He had sent his family across the Jabbok River. When darkness fell, suddenly he found himself locked in mortal combat with a stranger. They wrestled until daybreak, neither one the victor. Jacob was wounded in the thigh, but he kept on fighting. His adversary begged, "Let me go. It is almost morning."

Wounded, his night spent in unrelenting struggle, Jacob replied, "I will not let you go, unless you bless me."

The stranger responded, "What is your name?"

"My name is Jacob."

"Then no longer shall your name be Jacob, but Israel, for you have struggled with God and with man and have prevailed."

"What then is your name?" Jacob Israel asked.

"Why do you ask after my name?" his mysterious adversary replied, and he blessed him.

Jacob was wrestling with an angel. He knew not quite who or why, but he did not give up. He devoted his all to the struggle and held his own. By so doing he became more and more vulnerable. The word vulnerable means "susceptible to being wounded." Jacob was wounded, but still did not give up. Having pitched himself into the struggle all night long, he would not yield until his adversary blessed him.

By this final act of insistence, Jacob wrested meaning from what otherwise might be viewed as a night spent in utmost futility. Rising to the full height of his humanity, he struggled and prevailed, not begging God's sufferance but demanding to be blessed. And he was blessed. He showed the mark of his struggle for the remainder of his days, but emerged a new man.

Only one thing was denied him. Though he gained a new name—Israel, one who has struggled with God and with man and has prevailed—Jacob was denied the name of his adversary. "Why do you ask?" the angel questioned. Clearly, it could not be less important (Gen. 32:23–32).

Like Jacob, we each have our own personal angel, our angel of suffering and death. Locking us in mortal combat, this angel seeks to draw us too out of complacency, forcing us to confront ultimate questions of purpose and meaning, demanding that we awaken and discover who we are.

Religion is a peculiarly human enterprise, because we humans are the only creatures driven to explore the mysterious ground of their own being. We may not be the only creatures who know that we are going to die, but surely we are the only ones who wonder why we live. Many religions give final answers to these questions. Mine, like Jacob's angel, does not. In either case, by not giving up in our struggle for meaning, and in finally demanding to be blessed no matter what the cost, our name too is changed. We attain to our full human stature.

There is nothing easy about it. Jacob, victorious, was left with wounds that remained with him throughout his days. That is the price we must pay. The call of the angel is like the call to love. In rising to meet its challenge we become vulnerable. We must prepare to relinquish everything when we rise in answer to the angel's charge.

When we do, we discover that suffering, love, and mortality all come in the same package. Take away one, and you take away the others as well. Certainly you take away love, for it is impossible to love that which you cannot lose.

The angel of death does not wait by our sickbeds in hope of transporting us to heaven. Instead, she wrestles with us when we need reminding how vulnerable we are and how precious vulnerability is. And when we survive the crisis of awakening, we remember, as if for the very first time, that all our earthly cares are nothing when measured against the privilege of having them. We remember that any day in which we do not acknowledge in some tangible way how blessed we are in our loved ones, in the tasks we are called to do, even in the burdens we bear and trials we face, is a day squandered. Nothing could be more important. Yet, without death and the angel of death to remind us, we would often forget to remember.

How much better this is than wishful thinking. Perhaps, attending to the angel of death, we should think to wish instead for something a little bit closer at hand.

The courage to bear up under pain;
The grace to take our successes lightly;
The energy to address tasks that await our doing;
The meaning to be found in giving ourselves to others;
The patience to surmount things that are dragging us down;
The comfort to be taken in opening our heart to another;
The joy to be gained even in the commonest endeavor;
The pleasure of one another's company;
The blessed wonder and eternal possibility that lies between
The sacred moments of our birth and our death.

The angels have a name for it. They call it "thoughtful wishing," thinking to wish for what can be ours, for what we can do, for what we can be.

One other thing. Thoughtful wishes tend to come true.

When Skiageneia, daughter of Persephone and Pluto, managed to stow away in her mother's chariot on a brief visit to earth, she spent her "holiday of delight" on an island whose rocky soil was tilled from dawn to dusk by mortals whose burden and joy it was to live, hope, love, suffer, and die there. Upon hearing the muffled roar of Pluto, coming to fetch her back, she ascended to the highest point of the island and saw what we ourselves might see were we to look with open eyes upon our own horizon.

The island was hers, and the deep,
All heaven, a golden hour.

Then with wonderful voice that rang
Through air as the swan's nigh death,
Of the glory of Light she sang,
She sang of the rapture of Breath. . . .
She sang of furrow and seed,
The burial, birth of the grain,
The growth, and the showers that feed,
And the green blades waxing mature
For the husbandman's armful brown.
O, the song in its burden rang pure,
And burden to song was a crown.

6. Angels of Birth

The secret of the universe is a room where life is reborn out of death. A room where you are commissioned in darkness. A room where the white wicker rocker ticks and morning after morning you are given back the world. A room in a dream where you write out a name in the wet. This room where you are now, crowded with angels.

FREDERICK BUECHNER

Behold, I bring you glad tidings of great joy.

LUKE 2:10

Nearly a century ago, Francis Church, editor of the *New York Sun* and a shoestring ancestor of mine, received a letter just before Christmas from a little girl who did not believe in Santa Claus. His response, published as an editorial, has since become a classic. "Yes, Virginia," he wrote, "there is a Santa Claus."

He exists as certainly as love, and generosity and devotion exist, and you know that they abound and give to your life its highest beauty and joy. Alas! How dreary would be the world if there were no Santa Claus! It would be as dreary as if there were no Virginias. There would be no childlike faith then, no poetry, no romance to make tolerable this existence. We should have no enjoyment, except in sense and sight. The eternal light with which childhood fills the world would be extinguished.

Francis Church was not a theologian, but this is quite commendable theology. In fact, though it is highly unlikely that any newspaper editor today, even at Christmastime, would go out on a similar limb for angels, he or she could scarcely improve upon the same logic. It is an odd sort of logic, but Christmas is an odd sort of holiday. Angels appearing to shepherds by night as they watch over their flocks. A brilliant star illuminating the heavens. A pilgrimage of Magi. The birth of a child.

Christmas is an adventure into the land of parable and myth. Parables, like angels, are revelations of the divine within the ordinary. Myth is a projection of the temporal, the ordinary, the human, upon a cosmic screen.

Both tend to make people nervous. Especially myth. How eagerly it is abjured by biblical literalist and logical positivist alike. There is a fundamentalism of the left as well as of the right. If grounded in a radically different set of principles, the approach is similar. One thing positivists and fundamentalists share is a penchant for thoroughgoing rationalism.

Take the Christmas story. Both true believer and hardcore atheist test it for its facts. To the former they are absolutely convincing. Following the logic of one fundamentalist leader—"I believe that Jonah was a literal man who was swallowed by a literal fish and vomited up on a literal beach"—the scriptural record is read as an exact transcript of events as they actually occurred. The skeptic finds this incredible. And loses his faith.

Both forget that this is a story, not a historical record that will stand or fall only upon the facts. It is a story rich with mythic overtones and parabolic undertones, helping us set humanity in divine and divinity in human perspective.

One more thing. Like every story, its truth depends entirely upon its listeners. It will prove as true as love and hope are true, but only if it awakens us to possibilities for love and hope within our own lives.

We are back in the fields surrounding Bethlehem. Suddenly, the sky shines with a great light, an angel of God. We are terrified, but the angel says, "Be not afraid; for behold, I bring you good news of a great joy, which will come to all the people" (Luke 2:10).

What could be more simple or more startling? A child is born. The spark of divinity planted in animal flesh, incarnation, the miracle of human birth fixed at the crosspoint of the vertical axis, which is God's axis, and the horizontal axis, which is the axis of temporal as opposed to eternal things. "Infancy is the perpetual Messiah," writes Ralph Waldo Emerson, "which comes into the arms of fallen men and pleads with them to return to paradise."

With every birth something of eternity is made incarnate in that which is found by time. In this sense, Jesus' birth in the manger is archetypal. Not only does it prefigure our own, but also, in the bloom of its promise, the birth of the baby Jesus reawakens us to the limitless nature of our own possibilities. Placed within our arms, it pleads with us to return to paradise. Birth, joy, and eternity are here inextricably linked in a mythic pattern expressed within a parable, the child—a manifestation of the divine in the ordinary. No wonder it is shot through with angels.

If we don't always recognize them it's simply because angels often are disguised. Our children can help us here, for angels don't always come packaged in angelic guise.

Several Christmases ago, when my son Twig was three, we were walking past St. Vincent's Catholic Church in New York City, a highly ornamented structure on Lexington Avenue replete with archangels mounted on parapets blowing their trumpets. "Why doesn't our church have fairies on it?" Twig asked. Later that week, Twig was an angel in our

Christmas pageant. Shortly after singing "Away in a Manger," he fell asleep on the pulpit steps.

Not only our children, but our parents also. I remember one Christmas when I was just a little older than Twig is now. My father tried to disguise an incompetent tree by veiling its deformities in pink angel hair, a cross between insulation and cotton candy. Having molled this pathetic tree up as best he could, he turned on the lights and declared her, despite his best efforts and in part because of them, a sorry but hopeful strumpet past her prime. As I think back upon this, surely somewhere in heaven an angel gazed down fondly upon the tree and upon us, recognized herself in both, and laughed.

In the infancy narrative in Luke, angels not only appear to announce Jesus' birth, but his conception as well. And even before this, Gabriel, "the Hero of God," tells Zacharias that his wife Elizabeth, like Sarah a woman advanced in years, will give birth to a son, whose name will be John— John the Baptist. It is six months later that the angel visits Elizabeth's cousin Mary, and says that she too will bear a child. Elizabeth assures Mary that all will be well, and foreshadowing her son's proclamation concerning Jesus, tells her that she will be held blessed among women because of this (Luke 1–2).

Mothers and angels. They often come together in the Bible. Sarah, Hagar, Elizabeth, and Mary all have this in common. Their delivery is announced by a messenger of God. And with each delivery comes not only a child but also the promise of deliverance for other children: Isaac and Ishmael, each to father a great nation; John the Baptist, preacher of repentance and prophet of redemption; Jesus the savior.

Throughout the biblical narrative, it is these two messages that God's messengers bring: Delivery and deliverance. *Behold you will be delivered of a child;* and, *behold you will be delivered from oppression.* One message has to do with being born, the other with being born again: the former a singular, if emblematic, miracle of incarnation; the latter, a miracle of transfiguration, riddled with meanings that are shared.

First we are born, delivered into the world, which if not our oyster is our teat. When we enter into the world, everything around us is perceived as nothing more than an extension of our own being. From our first breath and well before, the life force that animates and sustains us is taken for granted. It is a given. As we grow through the pains of separation and ego development, and find ourselves having to compete for affection and shelter and sustenance, the complexities of the human condition become more manifest. But we may still continue taking life for granted. Lacking some kind of religious second-birth, we may follow this same path, even if in half-conscious flight from death, all the way to the grave.

At some point, awakening to the angels' song, it may dawn upon us that life is not a given but a gift: not something to be taken for granted and occasionally begrudged, but an undeserved, unexpected, holy, awesome, and mysterious gift. That it will be taken away, as suddenly as it was given to us, is simply one condition that is placed upon this gift, a token in earnest of its preciousness.

If our first birth is an unconscious passage during which the gift of life is bestowed upon us without our knowing, to be born again is to receive the same gift consciously, reverentially, with humility and thanksgiving. We then assume responsibility for our lives. We are not responsible for being born, but we are responsible for what we make of our lives, for how deeply and intensively we live. In return for the gift, we understand that the world doesn't owe us a living. It is we who owe the world a living: our own.

If our religion doesn't inspire in us a sense of awe at the wonder of being, it has failed us, or we it. Having received life as a gift, if we are not drawn to revere the presence of this same gift in others, there is something terribly wrong. And if, from that sense of wonder, we are not compelled to respond in some life-protecting, life-enhancing, life-affirming way, then we must go back and start over again until the wonder we experience proves itself authentic by the quality of our response to it.

But first we must awaken. The messengers of deliverance, always veiled, are often strangers and sometimes forbidding. But unwrap the angel's message, and there, shining in the midst of this most improbable sequence of miracles, is a goal. It is to live in such a way that our lives will prove worth dying for.

Think of consciousness as beauty, as the unwrapping of a flower in spring, a little epiphany that strips away our blinders and invites us to front our being with passion and praise. Spring is the most temporal, most ephemeral of seasons. It bursts upon us in a riot of color, buds and blossoms, crocuses and tulips. We are besieged by a beauty that we know will quickly pass.

Our lives are a little like that. Born with the gifts of touch and hearing and taste and smell and sight, for a brief time we delight in these things, or take them for granted, and then we are wantonly plucked from the earthly garden, or wither and fade in our own season, at our appointed time. But if, in the fullness of time, we open ourselves, our pollen is gathered and scattered, new life engendered, sweetness and sustenance spun like honey from the fiber of our being.

Admittedly, there are certain narrow advantages to remaining closed. At the price of a diminished humanity, we can jealously guard our own nectar. Risking nothing, we shall have nothing to lose, even when death calls.

Forget about others for a moment. Think of it in terms of enlightened self-interest. Few of us would consciously choose indifference over love, boredom over enchantment, superficial knowledge over wisdom. Yet the patterns of our lives route us in precisely this direction.

Every routine is a rut. As long as our wheels turn in the same groove year in and year out, we begin to think we know what life is about, which means we know nothing at all. It's a little like that story Cleveland Amory tells in *The Proper Bostonians*. For more than fifty years, John Lowell had oatmeal for breakfast every day. One morning, to her shock, his cook burned the cereal and discovered that there was no more in the pantry. "John," she said. "There isn't going to be any oatmeal this morning." "Oh, that's all right, my dear," he replied. "I never did care for it."

Over time we construct prisons for ourselves, places to hide where our illusions will be safe. It is a kind of death-row situation, lacking only the guard to remind us that we are sentenced to die.

What we need is a prison breaker. Scissors over paper; stone over scissors; paper over stone. Whatever breaks the pattern, not to replace it but to interrupt it. As if awakening us from a living sleep, drawing our eye to look anew at life and death, leading us perhaps to a deeper understanding of what it means to be alive and then to die.

When we entertain angels unawares, more often than

not the culprit is some cherished routine. Each of us has a bevy of them. We must to survive. The irony is that while we cannot live without them, we cannot awaken without breaking them.

The angels have a trick to crack the lock. They call it "excess in moderation." Its opposite numbers, both ultimately debilitating to the spirit, are "excess in excess," and another—with which I am somewhat less well acquainted but no less perilous—"moderation in excess."

As to the former, to be consumed by our passions is to be daily eaten alive and left for dead. We can fool ourselves only so long—the length of a lifetime, say. And then it is ended; not only the pain, pretense, and folly, but also the promise of deliverance.

Moderation in excess is different, and in a way more dangerous. When our life is out of control we are generally aware that all is not well. With this awareness comes the chance at least for an act of will to work a saving change and liberate us from the grip of self-destruction.

On the other hand, when our life is under complete control we are generally not aware that all quite probably is *not well*. Life flies by, days and weeks and years consumed by steady, predictable, unexceptionable routines. Such a life avoids death by disguising itself as death, an endless repetition, until the real thing comes along.

"There is always an enormous temptation in all of life to diddle around making itsy-bitsy friends and meals and journeys for itsy-bitsy years on end," Annie Dillard writes.

It is so self-conscious, so apparently moral, simply to step aside from the gaps where the creeks and winds pour down, saying, I never merited this grace, quite rightly, and then to sulk along the rest of your days on the edge of rage. I won't have it. The world is wilder than that in all directions, more dangerous and bitter, more extravagant and bright. We are making hay when we should be making whoopee; we are raising tomatoes when we should be raising Cain, or Lazarus.

Take Palm Sunday. Jesus was in danger of his life and knew it. As long as he remained in the hills he was safe. In Jerusalem the authorities were after him. He posed the threat of a disturbance. Their responsibility was to maintain order in the name of Rome.

And so what does he do? Allowing himself to be mockregally enthroned on the back of an ass, he proceeds toward Jerusalem, his motley followers providing all the trappings of a royal parade, setting before him a bed of garments and flowers, lining his passage with a flourish of fronds. By this single act, Jesus manages to ridicule the pretentions of both the secular and the religious authorities, having irreverently donned the mantle of "King of the Jews," and having made a civil disturbance. The first thing he does when he gets to Jerusalem is to go straight to the temple and overturn the tables of the money changers. In less than a week he is dead (Matt. 21–27).

When we risk nothing, we have nothing to lose. That is one advantage of the lowest common denominator. Nowhere to fall. But whenever we wish to borrow them, the angels will lend us their wings. Try putting them on. Fly a little too close to the sun. Take the plunge. The heights and depths are dangerous, but they do remind us of what it really means to seek and fail, love and lose, live and die.

Shall we continue "to measure our lives in coffee spoons," as T. S. Eliot puts it, or do what E. M. Forster suggests—

after six cups of tea, throw the seventh in the face of the hostess?

The angel of death wears simple clothes, but the angels of birth are distinguished by a touch of irony, a dash of anarchy, and a brightly painted, eye-stopping splash of exuberance. They urge us onward to unwrap our uniqueness, trump out our outrageous and diverse human finery, march like kings into the corridors of pretense and temporal power, disarm the hostess in some demure salon, wake up the party, redistribute the favors.

There are many ways to practice "excess in moderation." You might try what my father used to do—go to a fancy restaurant and bellow when you put your fork into a piece of rare roast beef—anything to keep awake. But it is then, once we are awake, that the true test comes. Jesus didn't march into Jerusalem to throw a party. He marched into Jerusalem to serve notice and die, not for himself but for others.

Each of us is born into this world in the natural way. We take our life for granted. It is our birthright. But when we dare to acknowledge it, we know that we must die. Until we are born again, death remains our master. That we reproduce our kind is not enough. If it were, we could be content to celebrate the cycle of the seasons. After winter comes the spring. Last year's death brings forth new life. But the world's great religions—Buddhism, Hinduism, Judaism, Islam, Christianity—promise something more. Each in its own distinctive way promises spiritual rebirth, bringing with it a taste of eternity.

When it issues in our hearts, sometimes this summons to be born again, is merely a passing fancy: a trifle to amuse us between pockets of emptiness. So long as the search continues on this level, we remain in bondage, no matter what novelty we seize upon with which to freshen up. The fundamental, almost unmentionable fact remains: We are wandering aimlessly, hopelessly toward death. Distracted by amusements, our daily tasks, our little lusts and self-consuming fears, we walk through the valley of the shadow of death, and God is not with us, his rod and his staff they do not comfort us. We don't even know that this is where we are, lost, wandering in the valley of the shadow of death, for it is all lit up like a gaudy, half-alluring, half-appalling Broadway marquee. The irony is that we live in hiding from death, yet know we will be caught; we sense that when all is said and done, our lives will turn out to be nothing more than a shell game in which we squandered all we had for little other than the barker's amusement.

When English novelist D. H. Lawrence was a young man he entered into a discussion of religion with his family pastor, the Rev. Robert Reid. A close friend of Lawrence's mother, Reid served a Congregational church in Eastwood, where Lawrence was born and raised. After Lawrence left home for school, his mother asked Reid to continue sending him sermons. The author's response to one of these— apparently a sermon on the necessity of conversion for salvation—survives. In part, Lawrence responded as follows:

I believe that a man is converted when first he hears the low, vast murmur of life, of human life, troubling his hitherto unconscious self. I believe a man is born first unto himself—for the happy developing of himself, while the world is a nursery, and the pretty things are to be snatched for, and the pleasant things tasted; some people seem to exist thus right to the end. But most are born again on entering manhood; then they are born to humanity, to a consciousness of all the laughing, and the never-ceasing murmur of pain and sorrow that comes from the terrible multitude of brothers. Then, it appears to me, a man gradually formulates his religion, be it what it may. A person has no religion who has not slowly and painfully gathered one together.

Here, in the lost yet familiar sermon of Mr. Reid and in Lawrence's response we encounter two very different notions of what religion is. On the one hand, there is the more traditional definition of religion, religion as a body of teachings and practices to which one conforms either out of habit or by a leap of faith. Faith here is predicated upon fidelity to the truth as it is taught. In most Christian churches this means accepting Jesus Christ as Lord and savior and the Bible as the unique revelation of God's word. Beyond this, there are specific requirements inherent to each of the various sects or churches. One group may affirm the central importance of adult baptism or Saturday worship, another the primacy of Rome and the authority of the pope. Basic requirements such as these are so common that people on the outside as well as those within such churches tend to identify religion itself with a subscription to some fixed combination of doctrine and practice.

Lawrence is talking about something altogether different. To him, our religion is formed through a process of encounter and response to the challenge inherent in life itself. It is something we slowly and painfully gather together, adding to it, shaping it, something which is never complete but which must continually undergo modification. When Lawrence talks of being born again, he is speaking not of conversion, but awakening.

The story is told of a Zen sage who sought enlightenment. Before practicing Zen he said he saw mountains and rivers. When he was engaged in his pursuit of enlightenment, he did not see mountains and rivers. Upon attaining enlightenment, he saw mountains and rivers again. Awakening is like coming home after a long journey and seeing the world—our loved ones, our cherished possessions, the tasks that are ours to perform—with new eyes.

Awakening is not only a term that applies to Buddhist theology. In much contemporary women's theology the term "awakening," rather than "conversion," is used to describe the discovery of what it means to be a woman and a human being in the fullest possible way. To use the old language, conversion means "stripping off the old man and putting on the new"; awakening means to discover oneself as if for the first time.

Think for a moment about the marketplace meaning of redemption. One has a coupon. It is worth nothing, or almost nothing, in and of itself. One-tenth of a cent, they say. But when we redeem that coupon, in return we receive something that does have intrinsic value. The coupon has value only once it is redeemed, translated into something of actual worth.

For us, redemption is not so different. In and of themselves our individual lives may be worth very little, 98 cents on the market, plus the gold in our teeth. But when redeemed they are translated into something of immeasurable value.

It is the ethical paradox. We empty ourselves and are filled. At its most basic level, this may simply reflect what Abraham Lincoln somewhere said about religion: "All I know is that when I do good I feel good and when I do bad I feel bad." But something more powerful is at work here, something akin to the proverbial planting of a mustard seed, yielding well beyond anything that might be measured simply in terms of self-gratification on a quid pro quo basis. In the words of Jesus, "The measure you give will be the measure you set, and still more will be given you" (Mark 4:24).

First delivery, then deliverance: To awaken to the eternal dimension of our time-bound existence; to search for meanings that go deeper than the skin; to liberate ourselves from bondage to the world of appearances; to enter the realm of God by giving ourselves away to others.

The old-fashioned Christmas spirit.

My accidental namesake and great-great-grand-cousin, Francis Church, really was a theologian.

You may tear apart the baby's rattle, and see what makes the noise inside, but there is a veil covering the unseen world which not the strongest man, nor even the united strength of all the strongest men that ever lived, could tear apart. Only faith, fancy, poetry, love, romance, can push aside that curtain and view and picture the supernal beauty and glory beyond. Is it all real? Ah, Virginia, in all this world there is nothing else real and abiding.

Or, as my colleague, Roy Phillips, puts it, "Christmas is real. It's the rest of the year that's a myth."

7. The Care and Feeding of Angels

I throw my selfe downe in my Chamber, and I call in and invite God, and his Angels thither, and when they are there, I neglect God and his Angels, for the noise of a Flie, for the rattling of a Coach, for the whining of a doore.

JOHN DONNE

The angels keep their ancient places,—
Turn but a stone and start a wing!
'Tis ye, 'tis ye, your estranged faces
That miss the many-splendoured thing.

FRANCIS THOMPSON

The D'Arcy Masius Benton & Bowles advertising firm recently published a report entitled *Fears and Fantasies of the American Consumer.* According to this report, three-quarters of us evidently have daydreamed about saving someone's life, and one in three about finding a cure for cancer. But when asked about our greatest pleasure in life, watching television tops the list.

We would love to be good it seems, so long as it doesn't inconvenience us too much. So long as we don't have to miss our favorite television program. But if we are unwilling to sell all we have to buy goodness, most of us *will* sell a little of what we have to buy a lottery ticket. According to the same survey, an incredible 70 percent of us do so at least once a month. Even more of us dream of winning big in the lottery. But the highest percentage of all reckons our odds of actually doing so to be no better than a million to one.

It's one thing to dream about being good, another to be good for something, but we appear to be especially good at simply dreaming. When asked about their "dream" job, men go in for adventure: professional athlete, test pilot, and race car driver are three of the top five. (Of less universal interest, but somewhat sobering for me, minister comes in fortieth of forty-four, well behind riverboat captain, spy, sex therapist, and dog breeder.) The top fantasy vacation for men is to go on an African safari. Women stick a little closer to the lottery, choosing a week of gambling in Monte Carlo.

The authors of this report conclude that "while the dream is of Indiana Jones, ... the life is much more Walter Mitty. . . . In real life, it seems that the closest Americans get to true adventure is watching 'Magnum, P. I.,' on the living room couch. While nearly everyone badmouths television, it holds an absolutely central place in people's lives."

In his parables, Jesus turns an interesting twist on hell. It is not so much a place where evil people are taken to be punished, but rather one where useless people are disposed of. There the chaff will be consumed, he says in Matthew 3; and in Matthew 13, Jesus describes hell as a place where the useless weeds must necessarily be burned. In fact, the scriptural word Gehenna, which we translate as hell, means Valley of Hinnom, the place of incineration outside Jerusalem where the rubbish of the city was burned.

After he died and before being elevated to heaven, it is said that Jesus harrowed hell. He entered hell, was tested by the fires, and emerged untouched. In like manner, but in our case before we die, we harrow heaven. Preoccupied, self-absorbed, too busy or too anesthetized to notice, we emerge untouched as well. When we put heaven "out there," or pine after what we have lost, or long for what we will never find; when we act according to our fears and not our faith; when strangers knock and we don't answer, we harrow heaven.

This is spiritual bankruptcy. In a world of riches we settle for five cents on the dollar. But unlike the parable of the talents, we do one thing the least provident of the three men—the one who buried his talent—didn't think of. We invest part of our nickel in a lottery ticket.

And yet we could sing with the angels. Should we fail to hear them singing, it is because our lives are too noisy. We are too busy to stop and listen for their song.

The word "busy" is onomatopoetic, a fancy Latin term for words whose meaning is expressed in the sound they make. Words such as business, busy, and buzz put us in mind of insects, especially bees and flies. Bees, of course, are industrious. We too sometimes are industrious. On the other hand, whenever I ask someone how she is doing and she replies, "Oh, I'm terribly, terribly busy," I think of flies. Someone—I think it was Mark Twain—once quipped, "The good Lord didn't create anything without a purpose, but the fly comes close."

I also think of chickens, modern chickens. These days chickens wear contact lenses—one supplier grinds out 150,000 pairs a day. The molded plastic lenses fit snugly over the eyeball, in this case not to improve eyesight but to distort it. Chickens don't run free in barnyards anymore; they are cooped up in crowded cages or poultry houses, where they are fattened for the kill. The lenses shorten their vision, so they will not become restive and rebellious, having seen the larger, freer world they cannot have.

Busy people are not occupied, they are preoccupied.

The word preoccupied literally means to fill our time and place before we get there. Much if not all unnecessary suffering is connected with such preoccupation, leaving us anxious, fearful, suspicious, nervous, and morose. For all our busyness, in fact because of it, we're always running late, with trouble on our heels. We do little but compound our insecurity, losing out entirely on that sense of inner freedom, a freedom that in fact could liberate us to act in ways that might allay the grounding for our fears. Since we are always preparing for eventualities, we seldom trust the moment enough to act within it. Our lives are filled, but not fulfilled. Even our guardian angels are left languishing.

You may remember the Old Testament story concerning Elijah at the Mount of Horeb.

A great and strong wind rent the mountains, and brake in pieces the rocks before the Lord; but the Lord was not in the wind: and after the wind and earthquake a fire; but the Lord was not in the fire: and after the fire a still, small voice. And it was so, when Elijah heard it, that he wrapped his face in his mantle, and went out and stood. (1 Kings 19:11–13)

An angel. A still, small voice. Amidst the turbulence of our lives, the tumult of wind and quake and fire, there sounds the call of a still, small voice. Name it what you will, the voice of God, the inner, healing voice of life itself. No matter, it is ever-present, beckoning us to stop and stand and listen.

It is nine o'clock in the evening. The children are in bed. I am sitting on the couch in my living room attempting to read. My eyes have tracked one page three times without connecting. I am distracted, preoccupied by the day's events. My mind is wandering. It covers a little ground then circles

back, half-attentive, locked in fresh ruts. Or it stops somewhere and spins. Vagrant images, many painful, steal into
my consciousness. "I should have said . . . I wish I had . . . Of
course, he didn't give me half a chance . . . but even so I
should have said . . . " Nothing unusual or earthshaking, just
the usual mix of unprocessed emotions, little haunting
memories and nagging thoughts. Just the old, familiar ever-
unfinished machinations of the mind.

It's hard to let go of anything that is ours, even those
things that sting when we refuse to let them go. Anger.
Embarrassment. Bitterness. Envy. Even the things we hate.
We hoard them like treasure. They constitute our case
against life.

Have you noticed how people tend to flaunt their grievances, almost as if they were a matter of great pride? As if
there were no higher privilege than to be numbered among
life's choir of victims. This is a choir unlike any other, every
voice a solo voice, singing his or her own sad music, oblivi-
ous to or even scornful of the human chorus welling through
the lot.

The victim's solace is perversely sweet, each bit part a
leading role, every diva with a rose. No matter that the rose
has thorns. Whether it be the solace of self-pity or self-
hatred, we are reluctant to ease its point from our soul. We
may not be so hard-bitten, but most of us remain reluctant
to cede our little place of privilege in the choir. And whenever we are tempted to feel sorry for ourselves, there is a
ready part for us. We close our eyes and stop our ears and
sing.

Just think of the number of times you have been reading
a book only to find yourself, as I did, lost in self-absorption.
On the other hand, have you not also lost yourself in a

book, lost all track of time and place, submerged yourself in its world, characters, setting, and plot, and emerged completely refreshed?

Or consider the times we have only a single important thing to do during the course of a given day. How difficult it is to wind ourselves up and just do it. The smallest thing distracts us. For instance, we set aside Saturday to pay the bills. So we brew a cup of coffee, read the newspaper, talk for an hour on the phone; the mail comes; we read a catalogue, fix lunch, take a nap, get up, straighten the study, make another phone call. And then do we pay our bills? No, we draw up a list of all the things we have to do over the coming week, placing "Pay the bills" at the top. By now it is time for dinner. We fix dinner, listen to the news, decide to pay the bills while watching an old movie. And maybe we do or maybe we don't, but in either case the whole day has been squandered in frustration. On the other hand, if we have ten things to do between breakfast and noon, among other things we get our bills paid. I have rarely heard a productive person say she was busy in response to the question, "How are you?"

Admittedly, the voice of a human soul is devilishly hard to keep in tune. With its interlocking registers of sensation, memory emotion, and thought, it is surely the most complex of instruments. Sensitive and therefore temperamental, it jams easily and at best is slightly out of kilter. Difficult to play well, it is impossible to play to perfection.

To keep ourselves halfway decently in tune, we must tinker all the time—here on our anger, there on our bitterness, lethargy, pettiness, or pride. Fully to love we must mute our fears; fully to serve, tone down our piping little egos. In order to produce anything like beautiful music, we must join in the band of our brothers and sisters, be an instrument of their peace, a humble instrument of justice and mercy, a dedicated instrument of truth.

To sing with the angels isn't easy. But there is a way to join our song with theirs. To bid for the angels' company, to beckon their presence, to care for them and feed them, there is no better gambit than prayer.

In prayer we sing by listening first. Prayer shapes and colors our melody, helping us keep in tune with ourselves. It also brings us into harmony with others. Finally, prayer tunes us to the cosmos, to the overarching and all-sustaining hymn of life. It recalls us to the symphony.

Prayer is the art of listening. Reverent attention to something unites us with it. Distraction divides, fragmenting us. Salvation and sin are much the same. Salvation—wholeness, health, healing, all words stemming from the same root—occurs in this lifetime when we are at peace with ourselves, united with one another, and at one with God. Sin is a state of brokenness. It exists when we are consumed by preoccupations and distractions, unattentive to the needs of others, at war with ourselves and the world.

The divisions within us spring from negative self-attitude based upon experience. We have done things we wish we had not done and left undone things that begged our doing. We have hurt others, letting them down and us as well. All of us have a weight on our shoulders that needs unburdening.

This leads us to the first of three kinds of prayer: confession. Jesus teaches us to love our enemy. How difficult this is if the enemy is another. Even more so if the enemy is us. Standing sentry at the portal of our minds, this enemy is ever ready to fend off the influx of better thoughts. How quick we are to remind ourselves that we have done wrong or been wronged, given or received pain, failed or been thwarted in our endeavors, missed out on some happiness or had it snatched cruelly away. The problem is, none of this does any good. Worst of all, we do not change, for the enemy within is a fatalist. "That's life. A pretty rotten business. Go ahead, stew. Given the circumstances, what else is there to do?"

At times, we tire of attending to the old carper. After all, was it not the same inner voice which, time and again, reveled in pointing out that, since we couldn't do anything about what ailed us, there was always the temporary expedient of oblivion? "Run, hide, get drunk, get stoned, watch T.V., bury yourself under the covers and then, however, much you toss and turn, don't get out until you absolutely have to." How varied and yet how very much alike are the diversions of the disintegrated personality.

The promise of confession is integrity. Confession is an honest confrontation with ourselves as we are. This, coupled with a faith in forgiveness, can heal us. If we dare to delve into our brokenness, confess, and beg forgiveness, the healing process will begin. Through confession, coupled with the will to change, we gain in strength and dedication. Having known what it is to be broken, we begin to discover what it is to be whole. Confession is a pledge toward wholeness. It cannot change the past, but it can help to bring the present out from under the shadow of the past. In this alone there is power.

A second kind of prayer links self to other, whether a person or a thing. At its most primitive, such prayer amounts to little more than begging for something we cannot have. Pray all we want for wealth or fame or happiness, in selfish prayer there is no power save the power of illusion.

But by keeping ourselves mindful of others, of their needs and the ways in which our lives intersect with theirs, any number of good things may happen. First, we are taken outside of our own narrow precincts. This is true of the simplest of prayers, "God bless Mommy. God bless Daddy." And grandparents and friends and pets and the moon! Such a prayer is a basic expression of connectedness. We become part of all we pray for, and it a part of us. Distances are bridged, our relationship to others becomes more organic, and thereby our wholeness is enhanced.

A more difficult example. We are estranged from a loved one. This estrangement has ever so many consequences which mar the present and darken the future. We are angry and so try to hide our anger. That is one classic case. Like an iceberg, only the tip of our coldness may show, but the rest lurks just below the surface. In such cases, those who are closest to us are sailing through dangerous waters. The most innocent maneuver may result in a collision. When we harbor bitterness or resentment within us, allowing our hearts to ice over, the slightest mishap may sink all hope for love. This is no way to live, either for us or for them.

Often our estrangement is the result of so many little things that it is hard to know where to begin unraveling it. Such estrangement tends to grow like a shopping list. The problem is, we can lose all sense of direction and never find the store. So the list grows, until we find ourselves carrying about a staggering inventory of grievances. No sugar, no cream, no warmth, no light. Late at night we tick off the items like sheep until they lull us into restless sleep.

For such a condition, no amount of mere accommodation will suffice to work a cure. An armed truce is no more than a reminder that the battle lines are drawn. Both of us remain on edge. We smile in company and lose ourselves, blessedly, in other things. But back on the home front, or in the office or wherever, neither gives ground without begrudging the loss, and neither gains ground without paying for the claim.

There is only one sure cure for estrangement. It is reconciliation. Reconciliation is not accommodation; it has nothing to do with compromise. It demands a change of heart, a radical refusal to be trapped by our bitterness. It requires that we remember that there is a bond between us greater and more powerful than anything that separates us: the bond of birth and death.

Though we have little power over what others think of us, we do have the power to free ourselves from our anger toward them. We picture them in our mind. And we pray for them. It is hard to hate and pray at the same time.

Reconciliation, with those we think we hate as with those we try to love, is a living symbol of that which, in theological terms, is called atonement. Atonement is, literally, at-one-ment, the redemptive uniting of parts into wholeness.

The moment we pray for others, our attitude toward them changes. And due to the relief we feel once disemburdened of our spite, the way we approach them will change as well. In certain instances, the only thing that stands between estrangement and reconciliation is an inability to imagine the possibility of reconciliation. In its very essence, to pray for another is an act of reconciliation. The image or possibility is brought to mind. Such prayer leads to a wholly different way of looking at others and our problems with them. We find ourselves looking through their eyes and not our own. When through another's eyes we see the same sun setting on the same horizon, we shall then know the bond that, in loosing all life, makes us truly one.

The third kind of prayer is the most healing of all. It is a way of saying yes to life, a yes of gratitude and trust. Blending all dissonance into a larger harmony, putting all the parts in perspective of the whole, we say, *I am in thy hands, thy will be done.* In such a prayer, we ask nothing of ourself or for another. We simply acknowledge life's wonder and mystery, not taking it for granted, but receiving it as a gift.

This is the most important of prayers, a loving token of fidelity to all that lies beyond our power to effect or change, an expression not of obligation but of appreciation, not of guilt but gratitude. It is a way of letting go and for a blessed moment being swept away. Without demand, beyond regret, we yield.

In the Psalms it is called the sacrifice of Thanksgiving. Not only do we sacrifice our ego in a sense—by acknowledging the receipt of undeserved gifts, especially the gift of life—but also we find our life rendered sacred by this same acknowledgment. Sacrifice means to render sacred. By suspending the claim of our own ultimacy, willfulness, and authority, we are freed to perform this sacrifice. The present becomes one with eternity. In eternity, division and brokenness are overcome. Where once we harrowed, we are hallowed and made whole.

We enter heaven.

8. Heaven in a Wildflower

Outside the open window
The morning air is all awash with angels.

RICHARD WILBUR

Everything I am about to say is both true and false. It is yes
and no at once, like one of those wondrous days, rarely
experienced but never to be forgotten, when the sky is blue
and bright and the rain comes pouring down—those days
that remind us that things are not always what they appear
to be. Looking for ourselves, we remember that until we
are lost we cannot be found. Struggling for meaning, we
remember that until we are empty we cannot be filled.
Seeking something in our lives that will abide, we awaken
to the fact that only those things we have given away can
ever truly be ours. And we look into the sun-drenched rain
and say to ourselves, even if God does not exist, we are
here only by the grace of God.

Let me tell you a story I learned from Catholic theologian John S. Dunne. It is the parable of the mountain.

One day a group of seekers begins to climb a mountain
in search of God. God, they are told, or something very
like God, lives at the top of this mountain. So they leave
their daily cares behind them—all the human cares of love
and death and war and suffering—and climb in search of
pure Truth, or Beauty, or Goodness, or Knowledge. In
short, they follow the signs that point to God, transcendent,
all-knowing, all-powerful.

Finally, they get to the top of the mountain. From the top of the mountain they can see farther than they have ever seen before. And the air is thin at the top of the mountain. This is conducive to abstract and disembodied reflection on the eternal verities, the very things that are confounded and veiled by the grossness and busyness and squalor of the all-too-human life below. There is only one problem. God is not there. While they were climbing up the mountain in search of God, God was climbing down the mountain into the valley. As the pilgrims seek escape from their human lot, seeking transfiguration into something immortal and divine, God's desire is to be human, to become incarnate in mortal flesh, to escape the everlasting emptiness of eternity.

Play with it in your mind.

We go up as God comes down. Each to the other is like a vanishing pot of gold at two ends of a rainbow. The mystery is that by reaching for God, for a divine hand that turns out not to be there, we may in fact be changed, saved, redeemed. And in seeking *us* out, who knows? Perhaps God too is changed. Humbled. Spun into webs of passion and stung with pain. Brought to life.

The idea that God lives on a mountain is a mythic idea. It goes back to the ancient Greeks and beyond. It is easy to understand why. If you were God surely you would want a lofty perch with an expansive view. Particularly if it was relatively inaccessible. After all, part of your power has to do with the awe in which you are held by mortals. There is only one problem with mountaintops, especially when one is immortal and therefore fated to live forever high above the clouds. The problem with mountaintops is that every now and then one tends to get terribly, terribly lonely.

It is then that one disguises oneself as a bull or a swan or a holy ghost and goes down into the valley below and fathers a child. This, by the way, is the stuff of which parables are made: The Kingdom of God is like a mustard seed; the Kingdom of God is like a babe wrapped in swaddling clothes lying in a manger.

Of the parables of the Kingdom, such as the parable of the sower or the parable of the woman at the well, the symbols here participate in the very reality to which they refer. Just like angels. The medium is the message, and both are God. Even as these parables are unpretentious to a fault, they invite us to look again at commonplace things within our own lives, beckoning us to view them not as they appear, but as signs of something deeper, more essential and abiding, insinuating into our workaday lives barbed and haunting questions that throw all we take for granted into a kind of divine abeyance. We are challenged to awaken from our mechanical daze to consider ultimate things. Not unlike the story of his birth or the story of his march to death, Jesus' parables constitute a frontal assault upon the dogma of the apparent. They remind us where heaven really is.

As Jesus himself says in Luke 17:22 when asked by the Pharisees when the Kingdom was coming, "The Kingdom is not coming with signs to be observed; nor will they say, 'Lo, here it is!' or 'There!' for behold, the Kingdom of God is in the midst of you." And in another version of this same saying as recorded in the Gospel of Thomas, he tells his disciples, "What you expect has come, but you know it not."

It doesn't really matter whether we are searching for God, or simply for some divine characteristic attributed to

God. And it doesn't matter if we find what we are seeking. Almost certainly we will not. What does matter is that we climb the mountain, for from the top of the mountain, we gain a new perspective on our lives. We awaken to heady and mysterious things. And when we quickly discover that we can no longer breathe the air, and return to the valley, we find that in our absence God has visited our homes. Loved ones we had begun to take for granted become again precious to us. Work we had begrudged is suddenly an honor to perform. Routine daily things sparkle with a new luster. Whereas before we were doing time, our lives living us, the sand unwatched running out of our glass, we now are awake to the unaccountable miracle of life and love and death, each precious, each ours to honor and affirm.

To paraphrase Saint Augustine's admonition to theologians who were driven to write about God, "If you can understand it, then it is not God." My colleague Wallace Robbins recast this same passage in contemporary terms. "Don't try to slap God on the back; you'll miss."

I like that. It is so like the way things are. So very like our going up as God comes down. For if by dint of extraordinary effort we actually do get to the top of the mountain, God is invariably nowhere to be found. Then comes the twist. Having failed in our search, when we go back down the mountain, returning to our loved ones and parents and children and neighbors, when we shake off the dust, put up our weary feet and look about us, like the Zen master we look with new eyes. Our lives, the very lives we fled in search of God, or Truth, or Meaning, are unexpectedly blessed with grace, for God has visited them.

I am talking about very little things. Touch that goes deeper than the skin. Shared laughter. A letter to a lost friend. An undistracted hour of silence, alone, together with our thoughts until there are no thoughts, only the pulse of life itself. I am talking about an afternoon spent free from worry about the things we have to do; or an afternoon spent doing things we have avoided. Both are somehow easier now. For we have been to the mountain. Though God was not there, when we return to our homes, our friends or lovers or plans for the evening or the morrow, and look about us very closely, we will discover that all has been touched by grace. God has returned to the mountain, but here in the valley we walk for a blessed time in God's footsteps. The ground we walk is holy ground. We don't really understand any better than before who we are or why we are here, but our lives become sacraments of praise.

My five-year-old daughter, Nina, entered kindergarten this year. She is going to P.S. 158, a wonderful old battleship of a school on 78th and York on the Upper East Side of Manhattan. She is learning how to add, how to read, how to spell. It is really quite extraordinary to watch. Every once in a while she writes her words backward or her numbers upside down. At first I cringed. Now, I simply admire. I have reawakened to the amazing fact that there are such things as numbers and words, and that she can learn them, and use them, and make sense with and by them.

Socrates once said that he was the most ignorant man in Athens. With each new insight came a deeper appreciation into the unfathomable mystery of being. Some people act as if they know everything. That is simply because their true knowledge is so limited.

Edmund Burke claimed that "where mystery begins,

religion ends." He got it exactly backward. Religion begins with mystery. And not only religion. "The most beautiful thing we can experience is the mysterious," Albert Einstein said.

It is the source of all true art and science. He to whom this emotion is a stranger, who can no longer pause to wonder and stand rapt in awe, is as good as dead: his eyes are closed. . . . To know that what is impenetrable to us really exists, manifesting itself as the highest wisdom and the most radiant beauty which our dull faculties can comprehend only in their most primitive forms—this knowledge, this feeling, is at the center of true religiousness.

If we do as Jesus said, become children to enter the Realm of God, we won't be able to number the angels on the head of a pin. Numbering is a grown-up game. But we will be able to dance with them in the ring of eternity. Children again, we may enter the Realm of God, but only through the gate of imagination. It is not so much a question of where to look for angels. The question is how. How to cleanse the doors of perception, to use Blake's term. How to see "a world in a grain of sand, and heaven in a wildflower." How, when we look upon the sun, to see "an Innumerable company of the Heavenly host crying, 'Holy, Holy, Holy is the Lord God Almighty.' "

I remember in seminary being told of the following religious experiment. The setting was a room, empty save for a simple carpet, a cushion to sit on, and a blue vase. The project director asked a group of his friends to drop by the room one at a time, morning, and evening, to meditate on the vase. Upon emerging, they were to write down their reflections.

After the first sitting, their comments were descriptive

of form and function. "I followed the contours of the vase," one person said. Another imagined it with almond blossoms in it, picturing it as a container," to which the director replied, "Don't do that sort of thing; there's far too much thinking going on; just meditate as it were on the vasishness of the vase."

After these somewhat mystifying instructions, they returned the next day and tried again. This time, their reported experiences were much more spiritual. "I felt as if the vase and I were one," or "I seemed to merge into the vase," the subjects rhapsodically exclaimed. So things continued for about a week. With each sitting, their religious experience heightened.

At the end of the week, the director removed the vase from the room. One by one they arrived as usual, went into the room, and discovered that the vase was gone. Many of them were stunned by a feeling of loss. "Where is the vase?" they asked, to which the director evidently replied, "Surely you don't need the vase now?"

During the course of this brief experiment, a blue vase had become for these people a numinous object, an object by which the sacred was made manifest, a little epiphany of the divine within the ordinary.

Just like angels.

Theologian Walter Wink defines angel as "the code name for the numinous interiority of created things." I like that very much—even as God is not God's name, but our code name for that which is greater than all and yet present in each, the vital power that infuses our being and folds us into its own. We will never break God's code, but angels are clues to follow. Angels are the DNA of God, the double helix of eternity.

Does that mean angels exist? Not necessarily. Even as it

is impossible to calculate the velocity and the mass of a particle in the same experiment, it is equally impossible to prove the existence of angels without leaving their realm. Like God, angels are beyond proof, at least in the scientific sense of the term. Once we start arguing about whether or not angels exist, we have already missed the point. Remember, the word angel is indicative of duty, not of nature. An angel is what it says and does, not what it is.

So the question is not whether angels exist, but what do angels do. Here there are as many answers as there are moments for awakening in any given lifetime. Angels awaken us to the wonder and mystery of being, laughing when we take ourselves too seriously, surprising us with the beauty of their strangeness, knocking on our door to deliver messages of death and birth. They are salt when we lose our savor, joy and pain when we've forgotten how to feel. Angels are metaphors. They carry us from one realm to another. They are "tongues in trees, books in the running brooks, sermons in stones and good in every thing."

Writing this book I have been far busier thinking about angels than listening to their song. Theology is a fool's game. The jester is the one who can offend the king without losing his head. But his eyes too will eventually close. Forever. Perhaps that is why the fool tries so desperately to speak the truth. Not to fool the king or himself, but to anchor things down in honest ground. For this there are no authorities.

But just below the surface something is glimmering, something that gives meaning to our lives and to our deaths. Begin with simple things. I can write and you can read.

Each is a miracle.

Angelic Blessings

Blessed are the poor in spirit,
for they know the unutterable beauty of simple things.

Blessed are those who mourn,
for they have dared to risk their hearts by giving of their
love.

Blessed are the meek,
for the gentle earth shall embrace them and hallow them
as its own.

Blessed are those who hunger and thirst after righteousness,
for they shall know the taste of noble thoughts and deeds.

Blessed are the merciful,
for in return theirs is the gift of giving.

Blessed are the pure in heart,
for they shall be at one with themselves and the universe.

Blessed are the peacemakers,
for theirs is a kinship with everything that is holy.

Blessed are those who are persecuted for righteousness'
sake,
for the truth will set them free.

Sources

PREFACE

9. **"Angels can fly"** G. K. Chesterton, *Orthodoxy* (Garden City, NY: Image, 1959), 120.

10. **"The reason Milton"** William Blake, "The Marriage of Heaven and Hell," in *The Complete Writings of William Blake,* ed. Geoffrey Keynes (London: Oxford University Press, 1966), 150.

10. **"That's all an"** Meister Eckhart, Sermon XXIX, cited by Theodora Ward, *Men and Angels* (New York: Viking, 1969), 121.

11. **"The word good"** G. K. Chesterton, quoted in *The New Book of Christian Quotations,* ed. Tony Castle (New York: Crossroad, 1984), 98.

1. HEAVEN AS HELL: HARPS, HYMNALS, AND HALOS

15. **"I want to"** Urania Bailey, "I want to be an angel," cited in *Encyclopedia of Religious Quotations,* ed. Frank S. Mead (Westwood, NJ: Revell, 1965), 5.

15. **"The angels all"** George Gordon, Lord Byron, "The Vision of Judgement," stanza 2.

15–17. **"I beg pardon ... go to church"** Mark Twain, *Extract from Captain Stormfield's Visit to Heaven* (New York: Harper & Brothers, 1909), 25–28; 37–38.

16. **"To equip a"** Robert Louis Stevenson, "Virginibus Puerisque: Crabbed Age and Youth," in *The Works of*

Robert Louis Stevenson, vol. 25 (London: William Heinesmann, 1924), 49.

18. **"I am discontented"** Maurice Sendak, *Higglety-Pigglety Pop! Or There Must Be More to Life* (New York: Harper & Row, 1967), 5.

19. **"angels are God's ... heavy artillery"** Billy Graham, *Angels: God's Secret Agents* (Garden City, NY: Doubleday, 1975), 43, 164, 15.

20. **"Man's heaven is"** Mark Twain, *Notebook,* ed. A. B. Paine (New York: Harper & Brothers, 1935), 397, 398.

21. **"While it's true"** Angela Devine and Rory Fellowes, *Heaven: A Guide* (London: Unwin, 1985), 35.

21. **"An angel is"** C. S. Lewis, *A Preface to Paradise Lost* (Oxford: Oxford University, 1961), 113.

21. **"What are angels"** White Bear Unitarian Church Newsletter, December 1985, p. 2.

22. **"A beautifully set"** Martin Luther, *Table Talk,* vol. 54 of *Luther's Works,* ed. Theodore G. Tappert (Philadelphia: Fortress, 1967), 416.

22. **"In general no"** Angela Devine and Rory Fellowes, *Heaven: A Guide* (London: Unwin, 1985), 33.

23. **"None sing so"** Edgar Allan Poe, "Israfel," stanza 1.

23. **"Jacob, did you ... as we wish"** Lester Sumrall, *The Reality of Angels* (Nashville: Thomas Nelson, 1982), 122–23.

24. **"I want to ... might suggest hell"** Charles Erskine Scott Wood, *Heavenly Discourse* (New York: Penguin, 1946), 40, 48–49.

25. **"I have spoken ... and an angel"** Emanuel Swedenborg, *Heaven and its Wonders and Hell* (New York: Swedenborg Foundation, 1960), 217–18, 28, 37.

2. WHY ANGELS CAN FLY

27. **"It is not"** William Blake, quoted by Carroll E. Simcox, *A Treasury of Quotations on Christian Themes* (New York: Crossroad, 1975), 37.

27. **"Too good"** *Talmud*, Shebu'oth, 15b, cited in Leo Rosten, *A Treasury of Jewish Quotations* (New York: McGraw-Hill, 1972), 256.

27. **"It is a"** Donald Barthelme, "On Angels," in *City Life* (New York: Farrar, Straus & Giroux, 1970), 129.

30–31. **"Who has not . . . not using them"** Montaigne— "That the taste of good and evil depends in large part on the opinion we have of them"—from *The Complete Essays of Montaigne,* tr. Donald M. Frame (Stanford, CA: Stanford University Press, 1958), 40–41, 44–45.

31. **"Obviously nothing can"** Sonya Tolstoy, *Tolstoy and His Wife,* ed. Tikhon Polner (New York: Norton, 1945), 139.

34. **"Miracles have ceased"** Ralph Waldo Emerson, The Journals and Miscellaneous Notebooks of Ralph Waldo Emerson vol. 5 (Cambridge: Harvard University Press, 1865), 423.

35. **"the comic relief . . . a beatific immunity"** Peter Berger, *A Rumor of Angels* (Garden City, NY: Anchor, 1970), 95, 59.

36. **"Do not indulge"** Marcus Aurelius, *Meditations,* bk. VII, no. 27, translated by Maxwell Staniforth (New York: Penguin, 1985), 110.

36–37. **"It is a"** Peter Marin, *Harper's,* vol. 258, no. 1545, Feb. 1979, 50.

3. ON THE SIDE OF THE ANGELS

39. **"Good kings who"** Elizabeth Barrett Browning, "Aurora Leigh," IV, i, 502–506.

39. **"Do you have"** The Rev. Jerry Falwell, interview in *Penthouse* magazine, vol. 12, no. 7 March 1981, 156.

39. **"If people enjoy"** *People* magazine, vol. 25, no. 6 Feb. 10, 1986, 107.

40. **"the native good"** George Santayana, cited in *Familiar Quotations* by John Bartlett ed. by Emily Morison Beck (Boston: Little, Brown, 1980), 703–704.

45–46. **"Monuments to the"** John Cardinal Wright, *Some Reflections on the Angels* (Boston: Daughters of St. Paul, 1979), 10.

46. **"for Church and"** Henry Adams, *Mont Saint Michel and Chartres* (Boston: Houghton-Mifflin, 1905), 1.

47. **"airy knights"** John Milton, *Paradise Lost* II, 536.

47. **"fierce fiery warriors"** William Shakespeare, *Julius Caesar* II, ii, 19.

47. **"On the night"** Arthur Machen, *The Angels of Mons; The Bowmen & Other Legends of the War* (London, 1915), quoted in the *Encyclopedia of Occultism & Parapsychology,* ed. Leslie Shepard (Detroit: Gale Research, 1984), 44.

47. **"because of the"** Harold Begbie, cited in The Encyclopedia of Occultism and Parapsychology ed. by Leslie A. Shepard (Detroit: Gale, 1984), 44.

48. **"When lo! an"** Wilfred Owen *Parable of the Old Man and the Young* (New York: New Directions, 1984), 42.

49. **"If this kind"** Mohandas K. Gandhi, *Indian Home Rule* (Madras: Ganish & Co., 1922), 96, 97.

4. ANGELS AND STRANGERS

53. **"without our eyes"** Plato, *The Republic,* book VII, paraphrased from a translation by Francis Mac-Donald Cornford (London: Oxford University Press, 1972), 231.
54. **"conducted himself so"** Martin Luther, *Table Talk,* xvii.
56. **"Calamity has come ... of collective punishment"** Albert Camus, *The Plague,* trans. Stuart Gilbert (New York: Alfred A. Knopf, 1958), 86, 87.
60. **"each one of"** Mother Teresa, quoted in the *New York Times,* Dec. 25, 1985, 34.

5. THE ANGEL OF DEATH

61. **"Life is so"** Attributed to Fra Giovanni and cited in popular media including greeting cards (e.g., Holly Tree Cards, Colorado Springs, CO.)
61. **"All God's angels"** James Russell Lowell, "On the Death of a Friend's Child," in *Lowell: The Poetical Works* (Boston: James R. Osgood, 1877), 88.
64. **"it is in"** Ralph Waldo Emerson, "Divinity School Address," in *Three Prophets of Religious Liberalism,* ed. Conrad Wright (Boston: Unitarian Universalist Association, 1983), 110–111.
65. **"Ten years ago"** Frederick Buechner, *A Room Called Remember* (San Francisco: Harper & Row, 1984), 187.
65. **"Death is not"** Billy Graham, *Angels: God's Secret Agents* (Garden City, NY: Doubleday, 1975), 150.
67. **"What sort of ... way of escape"** paraphrased from

Buddhism in Translation, trans. Henry Clarke (New York: Atheneum, 1972), 53–58.

71. **"The island was"** George Meredith, "The Day of the Daughter of Hades," in *The Works of George Meredith Memorial Edition,* Vol XXV. (New York: Charles Scribner's Sons, 1915), 59–60.

6. ANGELS OF BIRTH

73. **"The secret of"** Frederick Buechner, *The Alphabet of Grace* (San Francisco: Haper & Row, 1970), 101.
73. **"Yes, Virginia, there . . . would be extinguished"** Francis Church, *New York Sun,* Sept. 21, 1987, 6.
75. **"Infancy is the"** Ralph Waldo Emerson, The Collected Works of Ralph Waldo Emerson Vol. 1 (Boston: Houghton-Mifflin Co., 1903), IL.
79. **"John, . . . there isn't"** Cleveland Amory, *The Proper Bostonians* (New York: E. P. Dutton, 1957), 228.
80. **"There is always"** Annie Dillard, *Pilgrim at Tinker Creek* (New York, Bantam, 1974), 276.
81. **"to measure out"** T. S. Eliot, "The Love Song of J. Alfred Prufrock," in *The Wasteland & Other Poems* (New York: Harvest/HBJ, 1962), 5.
83–84. **"I believe that"** D. H. Lawrence, *The Letters of D. H. Lawrence* Vol. 1 ed. by James Boulton (London: Cambridge University Press, 1979), 39–40.
86. **"You may tear"** Francis Church, *New York Sun,* Sept. 21, 1897, 6.

7. THE CARE AND FEEDING OF ANGELS

87. **"I throw my selfe"** John Donne, "Sermon LXXX (at the funeral of Sir. Wm. Cokayne, 1626)," in *The*

Sermons of John Donne, vol. VII, ed. Evelyn M. Sempson & George R. Potter (Berkeley and Los Angeles: University of California, 1954), 264.

87. **"The angels keep"** Francis Thompson, "The Kingdom of God: In no Strange Land," in *Works of Francis Thompson,* vol. II (New York: Charles Scribner's Sons, 1919), 226.

88. **"while the dream"** D'Arcy Masius Benton & Bowles, *Fears and Fantasies of the American Consumer: An American Consensus Report* (New York: D'Arcy Masius Benton & Bowles, May 1986), 33–34.

8. HEAVEN IN A WILDFLOWER

99. **"Outside the open"** Richard Wilbur, "Love Calls us to the Things of this World," in *Poems of Richard Wilbur* (New York: Harvest, 1963), 64.

99. **"Parable of the Mountain"** John S. Dunne, *The Way of All the Earth* (New York: MacMillan, 1972), 14–23, 221–23.

102. **"If you can"** paraphrased from St. Augustine, Confessions, Bk I, ch. 1.

104. **"The most beautiful"** Albert Einstein, cited in Carl Sagan, *Broca's Brain* (New York: Random House, 1974), 301.

104. **"a world in"** William Blake, "Auguries of Innocence," in *William Blake's Writings,* vol. 2, ed. G. B. Bentley, Jr. (Oxford: Oxford University Press, 1978), 1312.

104. **"an Innumerable company"** William Blake, "A Vision of the Last Judgement," in *The Complete Writings of William Blake,* ed. Geoffrey Keynes (London: Oxford University, 1966), 617.

105. **"the code name"** Walter Wink, *Unmasking the Powers* (Philadelphia: Fortress, 1986), 169.

106. **"tongues in trees"** William Shakespeare, *As You Like It* IV, iii, 83.